Joseph Carroll Jeter

Adalbert Stifter's *Bunte Steine*

An Analysis of Theme, Style, and Structure in Three Novellas

PETER LANG
New York • Washington, D.C./Baltimore
Bern • Frankfurt am Main • Berlin • Vienna • Paris

Library of Congress Cataloging-in-Publication Data

Jeter, Joseph Carroll.
Adalbert Stifter's Bunte Steine: an analysis of theme, style,
and structure in three novellas/Joseph Carroll Jeter.
p. cm. — (Austrian culture; vol. 18)
Includes bibliographical references and index.
1. Stifter, Adalbert, 1805–1868. Bunte Steine. I. Title. II. Series.
PT2525.B863J48 833'.7—dc20   94-47006
ISBN 0-8204-2730-6
ISSN 1054-058X

Die Deutsche Bibliothek-CIP-Einheitsaufnahme

Jeter, Joseph Carroll:
Adalbert Stifter's Bunte Steine: an analysis of theme, style, and structure in
three novellas/Joseph Carroll Jeter. – New York; Washington, D.C./Baltimore;
Bern; Frankfurt am Main; Berlin; Vienna; Paris: Lang.
(Austrian culture; Vol. 18)
ISBN 0-8204-2730-6
NE: GT

Cover design by James F. Brisson.

The paper in this book meets the guidelines for permanence and durability
of the Committee on Production Guidelines for Book Longevity
of the Council of Library Resources.

© 1996 Peter Lang Publishing, Inc., New York

All rights reserved.
Reprint or reproduction, even partially, in all forms such as microfilm,
xerography, microfiche, microcard, and offset strictly prohibited.

Printed in the United States of America.

—in memory of Linda,
in honor of Gabriel—

Acknowledgements

The author wishes to convey his gratitude to the following people for their respective parts in the inception and preparation of this book.—General but heartfelt thanks to my parents, Vernon and Velma, for a lifetime of love and support.—An affectionately respectful word of appreciation to my former mentor in *Germanistik*, Professor Ursula Ritzenhoff.—A sincere thank you to the editorial and production staffs at Peter Lang Publishing for their patiently professional advisements; also in this regard thanks to Mr. Jean Perreault, Reference Librarian "emeritus" at the University of Alabama in Huntsville.

I wish to express a separate acknowledgement of especial indebtedness and gratitude to Priscilla Abbott. Without her critical and technical expertise, and without her unflagging goodwell, all would literally have come to naught.

Huntsville, July 1, 1995

Contents

I	**Introduction**	1
	The Origin of Problems in the Criticism and Interpretation of *Bunte Steine*	1
	A Survey of *Bunte Steine* Criticism	2
	Thesis, Methodology, and Scope of this Book	17
II	**"Granit"**	23
III	**"Kalkstein"**	57
IV	**"Katzensilber"**	111
V	**Conclusion**	177
	Bibliography	181
	Index	185

Chapter I

Introduction

The Origin of Problems in the Criticism
and Interpretation of *Bunte Steine*

IN 1853 A COLLECTION of six novellas by Adalbert Stifter appeared under the title *Bunte Steine*.[1] The stories are: "Granit," a tale of youthful mischance and reconciliation; "Kalkstein," the study of an idealistic eccentric; "Turmalin," the "dark jewel" of the collection; "Bergkristall," a Christmas tale; "Katzensilber," a story about a mysterious Gypsy child; and "Bergmilch," a romantic vignette from the end of the Napoleonic era in Austria. Although the collection was ostensibly intended to be a Christmas offering to children everywhere, it was not published in time for the holiday season of 1852 and appeared the following year. It is obvious, even upon a preliminary reading of *Bunte Steine*, that although the stories involve children to various degrees, they are not truly children's literature. Other editorial ambiguities concerning the collection stem from Stifter's choice of these particular six novellas from among the many works he had already published. All the stories, with the exception of "Katzensilber," had appeared earlier under different titles in various magazines and almanacs. The earlier versions were revised, in many places quite extensively, for *Bunte Steine*, and each novella was given as its title the name of a stone or mineral.

The fact that Stifter chose to put precisely these six tales into one collection and to give them geological terms as titles seems to imply that there must be some common element which links them together, but, paradoxically, the introduction and preface which Stifter wrote for the collection in the fall of 1852, before its publication, both support and complicate this assumption. In his famous "Vorrede" [Preface] to *Bunte Steine*, Stifter outlines in general philosophical terms his existential and artistic orientation and sets forth "das sanfte Gesetz" ["the gentle law"] of positive, natural development, which affects not only the individual but also social entities, nations and even groups of nations. Stifter's pronouncements, as stated in the Preface, are implicitly applicable to all of Stifter's work, however, and critics have found it difficult to ascertain and clearly demonstrate how the "gentle law" applies to the six novellas in the collection.

In his "Einleitung" [Introduction] to *Bunte Steine*, which was written during the same period as the Preface, Stifter directs his comments specifically to the six novellas and terms them a handful of "colored stones" which should be examined and arranged according to the reader's own insights and perceptions. This invitation seems to stress that the six tales are quite varied in structure, style and theme—which indeed they are—and thus to contradict, or at least render problematical, the compositional unity of them which is expressed in their titles and is implied in the Preface. Nevertheless critics have consistently sought a significant "common denominator" for the novellas of *Bunte Steine* almost since the collection first appeared. Following is a general survey of the Stifter criticism which has attempted to come to grips with this problem and an outline of the way in which this particular study will approach it.

A Survey of *Bunte Steine* Criticism

In 1974 Margaret Gump noted that bibliographic entries devoted to Stifter numbered some 6,200 items.[2] A perusal of such annual bibliographies as that of the Modern Language Association indicates that Stifter scholarship since then has maintained a consistent and substantial level of output. Sigfrid Hoefert, who outlined the historical development of Stifter criticism, states that other than a lively but fairly localized interest on the part of Stifter's immediate contemporaries, critical attention to his works was minimal during the last several decades of the nineteenth century.[3] Thanks chiefly to Nietzsche's high praise of Stifter around the turn of the century and to the efforts of some literary historians writing in the 1920's and 1930's, his works have gained steadily in

Introduction 3

recognition. With such notable exceptions as Ernst Bertram's *Studien zur Adalbert Stifters Novellentechnik*,[4] the tone and scope of Stifter criticism has progressed generally from biographically and philosophically oriented works of substantial length to shorter, more technically incisive studies of individual works and of such elements as structure and style. This general dichotomization into longer and shorter critical works has created some interesting interpretive paradoxes and a variety of analytical insights. The following necessarily selective but representative sampling should illuminate this situation and identify those major points on which most scholars agree. (Several additional pertinent studies are listed in the end bibliography.)

Ironically, it is the book-length studies and longer articles which often seem to create the most confusion. Although they tend naturally to treat Stifter's individual works only superficially, there seem to be occasional instances in such broad-based works of including, with frequently unsatisfactory results, detailed textual analyses of the sort one finds in shorter studies. This can even be seen in such worthy studies as those by Hermann Boeschenstein, Eda Sagarra, and Gustav Konrad. Boeschenstein,[5] for example, declares the essential critical problem of *Bunte Steine* to be an "unresolved residue" of tragedy in some of the novellas despite "no lack of regard for the gentle law."[6] But he then cites "Bergkristall, " one of the novellas which ends happily, to support his otherwise correct questioning of Stifter's "gentle law" as defined in the Preface to *Bunte Steine*. One feels certain that "Katzensilber," "Turmalin," or perhaps even "Kalkstein," should have been cited in this context instead. Sagarra perceives the same discrepancy between the programmatic espousal of the "gentle law" and the tragic tone of several of the novellas.[7] But she too sets forth a textually debatable view when she cites "Turmalin" as one of several exemplars in the collection which depict the ennobling effect of intense suffering. Konrad alludes to the potential inadequacy of philosophical Stifter interpretations and uncritical veneration of Stifter ["weltanschauliche Stifter-Interpretationen und unkritische Stifter-Verehrung"], but then he himself is guilty of the critical ambivalence which characterizes a great many analyses of *Bunte Steine*.[8] He asserts that the significance of the collection rests in the fact that the individual novellas show everywhere the dispensation of the "gentle law." But a few lines later he qualifies his agreement by suggesting that *Bunte Steine* must be considered interpretively in two distinct groupings, with "Katzensilber" ranged against "Granit" and "Kalkstein," as presenting thematic questions which are outside the sphere of an unconscious realization of the "gentle law." This comment reflects the difficulty scholars have experienced in finding a common thematic denominator for the six novellas.

It should be stated here that the studies cited above are, in fact, several of a large number of legitimate critical works devoted to *Bunte Steine* which, although unable to satisfactorily resolve the question of the collection's underlying unity, nonetheless contribute valid insights into the problem. Sagarra, for example, proposes such interesting ideas as a patently negligible connection between political and personal events in Stifter's life on one hand and his artistic production on the other.[9] She goes so far as to declare that Stifter either ignored or misunderstood the contemporary influence of the "Junges Deutschland" writers during the "Vormärz" in Vienna and that he was preoccupied with writing and rewriting in the interest of his "high ideals on art and its function in the community," and of promoting "permanent moral and aesthetic values in an age of change." Sagarra also provides such interesting and pertinent biographical details as Stifter's uncharacteristically vehement disapproval of Ludwig Richter's illustrations for the original edition of *Bunte Steine*. She states that Stifter was enraged by the depictions of angelic children and benign old men "as being wholly foreign to the idea of the tales." But additional citations by Sagarra, such as the assessments of Stifter's symbolic power by such figures as Nietzsche, Rilke, and Mann, seem to imply that an encompassing philosophical base for the collection does exist.

The ambivalence of critics towards the six novellas seems clear: should the novellas be considered critically as separate artistic productions or as integrated parts of a literary cycle? Although those studies which focus on Stifter's work exclusively show an even more pronounced ambivalence, they do surpass in analytical concentration those studies devoted to a genre or an epoch and hence can provide a better overview of Stifter's apparent philosophical orientations.

Introduction

The scope of these studies is still so broad, however, as to render impossible an adequate explication of the individual works. Even such a worthy and respected effort as Eric A. Blackall's *Adalbert Stifter: A Critical Study*[10] is not flawless in this regard. Blackall begins the section of his book devoted to *Bunte Steine* with the assertion that the political events of 1848 had an influence on Stifter's writing. He states that the work becomes urgent and programmatic and that there existed at this point in Stifter's career a real danger that a homiletic orientation might come to dominate his artistic impulse.[11] Blackall then declares, however, that no excessive didacticism mars the beauty of the *Bunte Steine*. These somewhat contradictory assessments are symptomatic of the critical confusion which arises when one attempts to integrate *Bunte Steine* too narrowly into a particular "*Weltanschauung*." But there is again an intimation here, at least, of a possible new approach to the collection. Other broad analytical statements by Blackall, such as his assessment that *Bunte Steine* is a collection of tales dealing mainly with simple people and children, fails to accommodate such complex characters as the enigmatic "brown girl" in "Katzensilber" and the eccentric priest in "Kalkstein," not to mention the adult figures in "Turmalin" and "Bergmilch." His assertion in the same context that "Granit" is chiefly the story of a family of pitch distillers does not give due consideration to the compositional complexity and thematic importance of the frame narrative. This oversimplification of the thematic interrelatedness of the frame narrative and the inner narrative continues with judgments that the pitch distiller's family is part of the spiritually bankrupt society which an outbreak of plague has created and that the people of the frame narrative are unquestioningly cognizant of the divine justice which befalls "these heartless people." A line-by-line analysis of the passages to which these comments refer indicates that the pitch distiller has removed his hirelings as well as his family to the wilderness, in part from his sense of responsibility as clan leader. His own brother, who chooses to remain behind, supports his action by agreeing to signal with smoke fires the termination of the danger. As to the didactic impact on the frame narrative of this "tempting of God," the Grandfather figure mentions the indifference of the contemporary generation to the preservation of the plague monuments and also points out that his neighbor, the weaver, is consistently breaking the Sabbath ("Granit" 34, 38). In fact, a concentrated analysis of "Granit" in this regard would indicate that the religious tenet most relevant to the overall narrative is the consideration of what the grandfather designates as the many strange fates awaiting people in God's world ("Granit" 25)—an idea more in keeping with the variety of plots, characterizations, and resolutions throughout the entire collection. Blackall correctly perceives the dominant stylistic pattern of "Granit" as being image-centered, citing the "extraordinary expressiveness of the language" as a "lyrical tissue of images . . . ."[12] But immediately he intuits a deeper structural complexity and asserts that "the elaboration of detail is more epic than lyrical." Blackall is very close here to recognizing one of the key compositional techniques in *Bunte Steine* as a whole: the duplicative use of imagery, of structural juxtaposition, and of connotative stylistic choices, to create a consistent thematic interplay which is nonetheless variegated in subtle but clearly recognizable narrative outlines. His schematized analyses of "Kalkstein" and "Katzensilber" however also point up the need for a closer scrutiny of the texts to ascertain the essence of that thematic interplay.

Also according to Blackall, the poor pastor in "Kalkstein" devotes himself as a youth to preparation for the priesthood in order to compensate for having a poor head for business. This lack of commercial aptitude is also offered as an obvious reason why he does not have enough money to implement his last will and testament. A line-by-line study of the text shows the matter to be much more subtle, in that the pastor's youthful eccentricity extends to all facets of productive social interaction, and his entry into the religious order is somewhat abrupt and undertaken when he is in an oppressed state of mind after the death of his last living relative ("Kalkstein" 108). One reason why his final estate is small is that he was robbed three separate times, but his business acumen ironically seems to have increased in his later years, as is demonstrated by his sound investments in orphans' insurance. Even such innocuous oversights by Blackall as his depiction of the poor pastor carrying the "Kar" children across the river in his arms (the text actually describes how he stands in a hidden depression in the swollen riverbed and directs the children to cross on their own) subtly distorts the positive but still imaginally egocentric nature of the cleric's actions ("Kalkstein" 79). It is again indicative of the paradoxical ambivalence prevalent in such generalized analyses that Blackall adopts a posture of specific textual scrutiny when he admits later that "Kalkstein" exhibits "a delicate restraint and tact."

Blackall's treatment of "Katzensilber" seems to reveal the same problematic attempt to combine broad interpretive pronouncements with analyses of isolated passages from the text. He perceives the construction of "Katzensilber" as "much looser" than that of "Kalkstein" and calls it a fairy tale which scorns logic.[13] He supports his assessment by describing the tearful admission by the "brown girl" at the end of the novella that "Sture Mure" and "der hohe Felsen" are both dead, as part of the "unfathomable poetry of nature." In the context of the thematic development of the tale, however, this obituary is the girl's clear expression of a natural sense of familial and even ethnic continuity. Blackall goes on to criticize what he sees as the grafting on to this "beautiful poem of nature" of an "ulterior purpose." Citing the first part of the work as a "fine piece of sustained writing," he views the second part as merely "a later visit to the same district," which centers on the "melodramatic and sensational" narrative of a fire and a rescue by the story's heroine. Blackall ends his critique of *Bunte Steine* with a bold but plausible declaration that Stifter's "conscious intention" was for the collection to be "an artistic and emotional counterblast" to the evils of the time.[14] While he admits the disputed thesis of the Preface, Blackall nonetheless sees the collection as an artistic attempt to preserve the socially progressive aspects of the politically revolutionary period which immediately preceded the publication of *Bunte Steine*. Such a view accords fairly well with the thematic content of "Granit"; but the characters and events in "Kalkstein" and "Katzensilber" seem to suggest an intent to vary and expand the basic outlines of Stifter's "gentle law" with an eye toward evoking a better understanding of its universal scope.

In *Adalbert Stifter: Deutungen*,[15] Konrad Steffen like other authors of book-length critiques focuses only sporadically on passages from the individual works in order to support broad philosophical pronouncements, but his incisive consideration of Stifter's youth and education does form the basis for a convincing interpretation of *Bunte Steine*. He recognizes the complexity and realism of Stifter's view of nature as an adjunct to his artistic interest in the varied destinies of humankind. He also offers support for an appreciation of Stifter's thematic configurations when he relates Stifter's life to his works, such as when he notes the similarity of the grandmother figure in "Katzensilber" to Stifter's own paternal grandmother who was also fond of telling tales and citing biblical parallels to everyday situations. This view of the old woman seems more valid than the harsher interpretations of her by some more recent critics.[16] There is also a relevant similarity between "das braune Mädchen" ["the brown girl"] and Stifter in his youth, whom Steffen depicts as a country lad who achieves successful integration into the cultured world of the Kremsmünster Gymnasium through his competence in natural sciences. Steffen's view is that Stifter's dual tendencies toward delight in the world of the senses and a yearning for transcendence ["Sinnenfreudigkeit und Verlangen nach Überhöhung"][17] reached its greatest artistic internalization and depth in *Bunte Steine*. This view fits well with the philosophical pronouncements in the Preface of a pervasive human impulse towards beneficent development ("Vorrede" 9). Such a view can readily encompass a thematic concept like dual existential orientations. But perhaps the most insightful of all of Steffen's statements is contained in the following observation: "Auf der Besiegung des Vitalen durch den Geist und der Begrenzung des Geistes durch das Vitale, ohne daß die eine Gewalt je die andere vernichtet oder um ihre Natur bringt, darauf beruht Stifters Zusammenhang mit der Klassik ...."[18] Although meant in a broad, philosophical context this view comprises two of the central components of the common thematic interplay which this study proposes for *Bunte Steine* as an integrated artistic production: "ego" and "socialization." It also forms a logical basis for Steffen's further belief that after the events of 1848 Stifter's most preoccupying artistic and philosophical concern was how the human being becomes a human being and remains a human being ["wie der Mensch zum Menschen werde und Mensch bleibe"].[19] Before analyzing the novellas individually, Steffen also provides an indirect parallel to the methodology which this book will follow: he describes Stifter, the painter, sitting before a canvas hour after hour, scrutinizing each compositional detail under a glass. Since it is known from Stifter's correspondence with his publisher Heckenast that he approached his writing in the same manner, at least from the early 1840's on, a similar line-by-line analysis may very well prove most fruitful in shedding new critical light on *Bunte Steine*.

The several interpretive discrepancies one finds in the brief individual analyses by even this most insightful reviewer of the collection are once again indicative of the peculiar critical problems which arise when one juxtaposes partial text analyses with biographical and philosophical discussions. Steffen begins his section on *Bunte Steine*[20] with the general statement that the collection exhibits almost exclusively the growing power of youth ["fast ausschließlich die aufsteigende Kraft der Jugend"]. This thematic aspect may indeed be present to some degree in all of the novellas, but it certainly would have to be relegated to only peripheral status in "Kalkstein," perceived only by contrastive implication in "Turmalin," qualified by extension into young adulthood in "Bergmilch," and granted sociologically problematic potential in "Katzensilber." Once again a critically recognizable generalization does not do justice to the thematic variety and complexity of *Bunte Steine*. The same objection could be leveled against Steffen's comment that Stifter's philosophical orientation creates an approach to fiction which concentrates more on a social continuum than on the individual member of society and his short life ["dem einzelnen Glied und seinem kurzen Leben"].[21] Steffen has clearly recognized the significance of such a continuum in Stifter's thematic scheme of things; but he does not balance that feature with the wealth of literary art in the novellas of *Bunte Steine* devoted to separate characterizations. Nor can his assertion that the collection depicts everywhere human beings under the sway of Providence ["überall die Menschen unter dem Walten der Vorsehung"][22] be as convincingly ascribed to "Kalkstein" as it is to "Bergkristall," if it can be demonstrated at all in "Turmalin."

Perhaps most unsatisfactory of all are Steffen's statements about the individual stories, such as his view of the characters and setting of "Katzensilber" which he describes thus: "In der Tat, auch die Personen der Novelle sind unsonderbar und gewöhnlich wie die Landschaft, in der sie sich bewegen."[23] It is true the characters do exemplify recognizable human types, but a close examination of the text reveals a noticeable amount of effective and interesting individualization for each of them in the context of their interaction. The carefully developed physical peculiarities and historico-mythical heritage of the landscape are essential compositional aspects of the thematic interplay also. The compensation which Steffen proposes for this supposed mediocrity is the permanence of the "Urgrund der Natur" [primal foundation of nature],[24] back to which the brown girl flees in the manner of Sture Mure and "das Wichtelchen" [the mountain sprite]. Such supremacy of the realm of nature does not permit the important thematic distinction between the continuum-based motivation of Sture Mure, who responds to news of her parent's death by returning to her native sphere, and the clearly mythical flight of the gnome, who may have actually left the natural environs altogether. The brown girl herself may be seen as merely better integrated into her woodland environment, in the manner of the pitch distiller's boy in "Granit," rather than as an embodiment of nature itself as Steffen asserts. Steffen indeed seems to recognize these ambiguities and returns to a valid instance of "Providence" in the wish of Sigismund in the story's closing lines for a good resolution for the brown girl. And he correctly perceives Stifter's intent that providence should here give life its meaning where nature and culture are no longer able to do so.[25] From the vantage point of his broad knowledge of Stifter's total work, Steffen explains this textual occurrence as a confirmation of Stifter's urge to maintain his equilibrium in the face of melancholia and unhappy experiences.

Margaret Gump's short biography of Stifter, although predictably general in orientation, contains some veritable gems of background information which she gleaned from a thorough reading of Stifter's personal, political, and professional correspondence. She offers such interesting observations as Stifter's complete faith in the ability of his mother (who was by and large an uneducated rustic) to interpret his works correctly, while confusion and misunderstanding often marked the efforts of more sophisticated readers. Such a view by Stifter of his own work could modify some of the more esoteric viewpoints which have been developed by other critics. A similar insight is generated by Gump's mention of Stifter's "other" niece and foster daughter, Josefine, who died of tuberculosis in the same year her emotionally disturbed co-adoptee, Juliana, met her death by drowning. A good case could be made here for a dual model for Stifter's brown girl in "Katzensilber," although most critics have assumed that character was patterned solely on the unmanageably fey Juliana. Josefine was by all reports a quiet, amiable child, and these traits are indeed discernible in the brown girl as well. Also a singular physical detail—the alien child's rosy cheeks, which near the end of the story become wan and sallow—has almost tuberculin overtones ("Katzensilber" 290). Hence, an additional complexity and thematic significance for that characterization can be reasonably suggested.

Gump's direct critical comments on *Bunte Steine* itself are also quite pertinent, if somewhat conventional at times. She alludes to the central position the collection occupies in Stifter criticism and correctly notes the paradox that interest is predominantly focused on the famous Preface rather than on the works themselves. She correctly sees the significance of the Preface as an explication of Stifter's "gentle law"; but she outlines Stifter's theory rather blandly as the correspondence between a gentle, slow-to-change, ever-recurring nature and the "unending daily repetition of seemingly insignificant attitudes and actions" in the human sphere.[26] She is much more arresting in her view of Stifter's thematic implementation and compositional manipulation of his theoretical base within the collection itself. She asserts that the underlying philosophical premise of the stories is the distinction between the development of the individual and the preservation of mankind, with priority necessarily given to the latter whenever a conflict between the two arises. But most importantly, she implies the modification of this view to include Stifter's "reevaluation of conventional values . . . revealed in the numerous repetitions and variations of this theme."[27] Rather than pursue an internal comparison herself, Gump chooses, as have numerous other critics, to amplify her views by references to earlier versions of the novellas later published in *Bunte Steine* and to at least one other author's work, Grillparzer's "Der arme Spielmann." This approach is, of course, quite fruitful for a biographical and philosophical overview, but its limitations in promoting a better understanding and appreciation of Stifter's artistry in *Bunte Steine* are evident in her assertion that "Katzensilber," the only original work in the collection, is most critically interesting in its development of a stylized "poetic monotony" which is fully realized in Stifter's later and longer works, such as *Der Nachsommer* and *Witiko*.[28] She cites with scholarly acumen Stifter's conceptualization of this design in his correspondence with Louise von Eichendorff, but she makes no mention of its pre-eminence in works which were conceived earlier, like "Granit" and "Kalkstein."

Before turning to a consideration of several more recent articles devoted specifically to one or more of the novellas in *Bunte Steine*, mention must be made of a little-known but analytically astute doctoral dissertation on Stifter: Israel Aluf's *The Concept of Integration in the Works of Adalbert Stifter*.[29] The breadth of Aluf's study, which combines both Stifter's total artistic output and numerous references to contemporary influences and which ranges from the legacy of Goethe to the works of Ibsen, renders it almost too general to be succinctly analyzed within the much narrower scope of this book. The fact remains, however, that Aluf was among the first of a generation of critics who attempted to interpret Stifter's works by examining what Aluf calls "a formal and systematic outline" of a single compositional element "in Stifter's Weltanschauung and in his work."[30] The (perhaps unconscious) priority hinted at in this declaration of intent causes Aluf to concentrate on numerous but necessarily brief textual proofs taken from selected works. Thus, although he establishes quite convincingly that the theme of human integration can be found in all Stifter's works, he finds it necessary to accommodate the negative manifestations of it in several of the works by ascribing to the author a gradually more conscious and positive development of this theme, up to its ultimate expression in his final works as the chief moral directive of mankind—

Introduction

"the gentle law." This developmental view is no doubt generally tenable, but its implications for an appreciation of the collection of six novellas in *Bunte Steine* are limited. In the first place, critics since Aluf have continued to perceive an essential dissimilarity among the stories and are able, at best, to group them into two or perhaps three different thematic sets. In the second place, if one considers the dates of composition of the stories, it becomes apparent that "Katzensilber," the last conceived of the six, employs a variation of the integration concept which is rich in artistic complexity and even ambivalence; but this variation is nowhere near as " developmentally" cogent, for example, as the one in "Granit," a work which was conceived considerably earlier. Also, when Aluf amplifies his concept of integration by aligning it with the depiction of "man's problematical and guilty self-assertiveness," he fails to take into account the complex characterizations of such "assertive" *Bunte Steine* figures as "the poor parson" and Sture Mure.[31]

There are numerous other generally valid pronouncements by Aluf on Stifter's *Weltanschauung* which seem, nonetheless, inconsistent with the characterizational and thematic variety in *Bunte Steine*. His view that familial membership is "the determinant of individual development and activity" does not fully account for the contrast between the twin brothers in "Kalkstein" or for the ostensibly self-actuated dynamism of the brown girl.[32] Aluf's view of the necessity of real wealth for a cultural continuum may be peripherally present, but it is not noticeably emphasized in "Turmalin" or "Granit." Also, his concept of nature as regenerative, sustaining, and representing an imperative integrative format for man is counterbalanced and even overshadowed by the depictions of its fury and man's efforts to regulate or exploit it in "Kalkstein" and "Katzensilber," and by its horrendous manifestation as plague in "Granit." It is, in fact, barely considered at all in "Turmalin." Stifter's supposed affinity for the peasant community as one of the "natural orders of society" seems ambivalent in the plague passages and the allusions to breaking the sabbath in the inner and outer narratives of "Granit." Hence, it is no wonder that Aluf, on those few occasions when he does cite *Bunte Steine* directly, asserts that Stifter's work is completely bereft of the "romantic conception of the distinctive, unique 'personality'." He then follows with such superficial character appraisals as "tragic" and "lonely" for the pastor in "Kalkstein," who in the final lines of that tale is clearly described as one whose life offers much inspiration for his fellow man.[33] To sum up, Aluf is correct in his perception that Stifter viewed the impulse of the individual to integrate himself into society as a universal one, but he does not balance this insight with other themes which seemed to be just as important to Stifter.

Some representative examples of the periodical literature devoted exclusively to *Bunte Steine* illuminate better the structure and style of the individual novellas. Such studies could provide a contrastive and comparative basis for considering the literary merits of the collection as an integrated and independent artistic production whose durability and popularity have assured it a place among the great works of German literature. Surprisingly, many of these studies have apparently yielded to the opposite temptation. Whereas the book-length monographs usually attempt to support general pronouncements by brief analyses of isolated passages from the texts, many of the shorter, ostensibly more focused analyses are marred by digressions which focus on the generalized interpretations of other critics. Some, however, do a fair job of striking a middle course. J. P. Stern, for example, manages to convey one very cogent insight concerning the stylistic element of Stifter's selected language.[34] Starting from the basic premise that "literature is incapable of conveying anything so abstruse as existence in and by itself," Stern nonetheless lauds Stifter's attempt at the unachievable and declares that this effort determined and dictated the narrative means which Stifter chose. Identifying the correctly-oriented reader of Stifter as one who can "bypass the complexities of the actual world" to perceive "the bare lineaments of existence," Stern credits Stifter's narrative language with facilitating that metaphysical detour "in a search for being itself."[35] As regards *Bunte Steine*, however, an intensive analysis reveals more an artistically unique interaction of that lyrical style with various depictions of life's complexities, which although perhaps schematic are nonetheless realistically outlined.

Donald Lo Cicero narrows the scope of his analyses to Stifter's relationship to the novella and presents a valid argument against those critics who concentrate their critiques of *Bunte Steine* on the incompatibility of much of the narration with Stifter's pronouncements of his "gentle law."[36] Lo Cicero contends that the predominance of description over action in many of the stories provides a life-like existential "border-zone" rife with dramatic possibilities. But his defense of Stifter's use of an inner narrative in "Granit" instead of a "Märchen" format does not take into account the complex and varied interrelationships of structure and theme within and among the six members of the collection.[37] There is, in fact, a thematically enhancing use of the "Märchen" technique in "Katzensilber"; and even Lo Cicero's claim that its use in that work is expressly isolated from the mainstream of the narrative is effectively refuted, as will be seen, by Eve Mason. Lo Cicero's quotations from the texts of the novellas also contain inaccuracies which are of interpretive significance. He does demonstrate an inclination toward a careful analysis of such elements as word selection; he notes, for example, that the juxtaposition of terms like "schwarz," "glänzend," "dunkel," and "seltsam" creates a mysterious mood in a particular passage. But his assertion that the pitch distiller's son in "Granit" later seeks out and marries the girl he rescued in the wood is simply in error and distorts the action of the story. It was the girl, in fact, who reopened their relationship ("Granit" 51). Likewise, when he asserts that the youthful eccentric in "Kalkstein" takes over his twin's business upon the latter's death, he completely ignores the fact that the future cleric served only as an explicitly passive "rubber stamp" to facilitate liquidation of the family estate in order to cover their outstanding debts ("Kalkstein" 107). By reducing "Katzensilber" to a tale about happy summers and daily hikes of a rich businessman's children, Lo Cicero overlooks completely the thematic significance of the Hof family's much more substantial and seasonally inclusive relationship to their country home; nor does he recognize the importance of the cyclically expressed relationship between the rural hill country and the urban center in the lowlands, with the latter and not the former apparently representing the site of temporary sojourns.

Eve Mason has examined how Stifter uses in "Katzensilber" aspects of the traditional fairy tale and she cites such similar features as contrast, repetition, and the use of clothing motifs for characterizational variation.[38] Mason sees this technique as Stifter's way of creating two separate narrative spheres, which she distinguishes as the supernatural and the profane. One wonders, in this context, if that dichotomy has not already been established by the paired anecdotes of Sture Mure and the "Wichtelchen" before the brown girl ever appears in the story. The characterization of the brown girl could thus be viewed as substantially more complex than just supernatural. Mason's interpretation of the girl's physical and judgmental precocity as supernatural also seems somewhat questionable in view of the fact that it develops gradually and naturally as the girl matures, as a line-by-line analysis of the work reveals. Also, the "almost stereotyped repetition" which Mason cites as the stylistic means to express this supernaturalness is also a notable feature in "Kalkstein"—a patently realistic work. Hence, Mason for all her interpretive astuteness, as expressed in the statement that the "selective" use of the fairy tale mode in "Katzensilber" forces the reader "to ask . . . the meaning of the whole story," impairs that inquiry herself when she assigns a morally punitive value to the probably commonplace occurrence of the house fire.[39] She declares that this catastrophe reveals some long-hidden psycho-social flaw in the world of the Hof. A more factual error is her statement that in the supernatural atmosphere of this story the children never skip or run as they naturally would. One need only review the passage describing Sigismund's first trip to the "Nußberg" [nut mountain] to find the perfectly natural individuation of such activities in the depictions of his older siblings ("Katzensilber" 232–233). Mason also shares Sjögren's exaggeratedly negative view of the grandmother in "Katzensilber," citing her "selfish" treatment of the brown girl during the storm sequence ("Katzensilber" 241–42).

There are a number of other studies which treat in varying degrees of concentration and incisiveness the six novellas in *Bunte Steine*. It is apparent from a survey of the secondary literature, however, that the central problem of *Bunte Steine* criticism is the difficulty of determining an interpretive principle common to all six tales, which can accommodate both Stifter's existential orientation on the one hand and the artistic richness and diversity of the separate tales on the other. This dilemma is nowhere more apparent than in I. E. Walter's "Hinweise" to volume two of the Bergland edition of *Stifters Werke in zwei Bänden*.[40] Walter insists that Stifter was able to write realistically and with variety, Hebbel's famous assertion to the contrary notwithstanding,[41] and he denies that Stifter was a person who did not understand people. Walter points out that in terms of conception and origin the six novellas lie far apart ["weit auseinander liegen"], and he proposes that all six share a pedagogical intent ["eine erzieherische Absicht"].[42] Remarkably, he admits on the same page a few lines later that at least one of the novellas, and perhaps the most famous at that, "Bergkristal," appears to be free of pedagogical motifs ["frei von erzieherischen Motiven"]. He suggests further interpretive difficulty by ending his remarks with an allusion to the widespread critical frustration with Stifter's slow moving plots, attention to detail, and prolixity ["langsamen Fluß der Handlung, die Umständlichkeit und Weitschweifigkeit des Stils"].[43]

Thesis, Methodology, and Scope of this Book

It is apparent from the studies considered above that a work which established a common denominator for all six novellas of *Bunte Steine* would be a legitimate contribution to Stifter scholarship. Surprisingly, there have been relatively few attempts to do this, and the few studies which treat this problem have for the most part appeared within the last twenty years. Paul Requadt suggested in 1968 that the unifying principle might be the "cyclical character" of novellas per se.[44] A few years later Helga Bleckwenn, who considers *Bunte Steine* a transitional work because of what she sees as its unfulfilled motifs, identified one such motif as "integration." Citing its occurence in "Turmalin" and "Katzensilber," she remarked that a dynamic polarity between this theme and an opposing one of "isolation" might well be the basis for a unifying interpretative principle.[45] But she concedes that a detailed study of the different ways in which the themes are treated in the novellas would have to be undertaken before the unifying principle which she proposes could be established with any certainty. What Bleckwenn seems to be recommending is a passage-by-passage or even, in some cases, a line-by-line analysis of the novellas which would uncover structural and stylistic similarities and contrasts common to all of them.

Careful study of the six novellas has led to the thesis for this book that there is not a single theme—or even two themes linked in dynamic polarity—which constitute a common denominator for them, but rather that in each of the six novellas three interwoven and inextricably related themes are treated in a remarkable variety of ways: (l) the ego of the individual human being; (2) the human society with which this individual ego interacts; and (3) the individual initiatives and actions which link the two together. In order to delineate these three themes and their relationships to each other, the method which Bleckwenn seems to propose has been adopted: a detailed analysis of the texts of the novellas as they appeared in *Bunte Steine*. Because time and resources have for the present made such an analysis of all six impracticable, three have been chosen which are seldom grouped together and seem to most critics to possess no pervasive, consistent common denominator: "Granit," "Kalkstein," and "Katzensilber." A careful and detailed analysis of the manifestations of the three themes in each novella will reveal both the unity which Stifter posits in his preface to *Bunte Steine* and the variety and variability which he suggests in his introduction.[46]

NOTES

1. All citations of the "Vorrede," the "Einleitung," and the novellas themselves refer to: Adalbert Stifter, *Bunte Steine: Späte Erzählungen*, ed. Max Stefl (Augsburg: Adam Kraft Verlag, 1960) 5–232. Any such citation not parenthetically identified by page number shares the page reference of the citation immediately preceding it.
2. Margaret Gump, *Adalbert Stifter*, Twayne's World Author Series 274 (New York: Twayne Publishers Inc., 1974) iv.
3. Siegfried Hoefert, "Realism and Naturalism," *The Challenge of German Literature*, ed. Horst S. Daemmrich and Dieter H. Haenicke (Detroit: Wayne State UP, 1971) 250–261.
4. Ernst Bertram, *Studien zu Adalbert Stifters Novellentechnik* (Dortmund: Ruhfus, 1907).
5. Hermann Boeschenstein, *German Literature of the Nineteenth Century* (New York: St. Martin's Press, 1969) 103.
6. This law apparently involved for Stifter a "welterhaltende" metaphysics naturally revealed in "das Ganze und Allgemeine," which ideally was to be implemented by a human ethic in which "jeder geachtet, geehrt, ungefährdet neben dem anderen bestehe." See the "Vorrede" 3.
7. Eda Sagarra, *Tradition and Revolution: German Literature and Society 1830–1890* (New York: Basic Books, Inc., 1971) 227 ff.
8. Gustav Konrad, "Adalbert Stifter," *Deutsche Dichter des 19. Jahrhunderts: Ihr Leben und Werk*, ed. Benno von Wiese (Berlin: Erich Schmidt Verlag, 1969) 366.
9. Sagarra, 224–31.
10. Eric A. Blackall, *Adalbert Stifter: A Critical Study* (Cambridge University Press, 1948) 257 ff.
11. Martin Swales, in his lucid study of the novella genre, designates this orientation as Stifter's engagement with "... the friction that results when the specific is pitted against the general ..." See Swales, *Novelle* p. 156.
12. Blackall 263.
13. Blackall 272. For a more detailed consideration of the fairy tale aspects of "Katzensilber" see Mason's article cited below.
14. Blackall 274.
15. Konrad Steffen, *Adalbert Stifter: Deutungen* (Basel und Stuttgart: Birkhauser Verlag, 1955) 7–52.
16. See for example, Christine Oertel Sjögren, "Myth and Metaphor in Stifter's *Katzensilber*," in the *Journal of English and Germanic Philology*, 86.3 (1987): 361–62.
17. Steffen 12.

18 Steffen 27.
19 Steffen 34.
20 Steffen 137–168.
21 Steffen, p. 139.
22 Steffen, p. 142.
23 Steffen, p. 160.
24 Steffen 163.
25 Steffen 164.
26 Gump 74.
27 Gump 75.
28 Gump 88.
29 Israel Aluf, *The Concept of Integration in the Works of Adalbert Stifter*, Dissertation, Brown University, 1958.
30 Aluf 16.
31 Aluf 10.
32 Aluf 62.
33 Aluf 55.
34 J. P. Stern, "Stifter's Fiction: '*Erhebung* without Motion'," *Novel* 1 (1968): 239.
35 Stern 240 f.
36 Donald Lo Cicero, "Stifter and the *Novelle*: Some New Perspectives," *Modern Austrian Literature* I/3 (1968): 20.
37 Lo Cicero 22.
38 Eve Mason, "Stifter's *Katzensilber* and the Fairy-Tale Mode," *Modern Language Review* 77 (1982): 114.
39 Mason 119.
40 Adalbert Stifter, *Stifters Werke in zwei Bänden*, ed. I. E. Walter (Salzburg, Stuttgart Verlag "Das Bergland-Buch," 1953) II: 7.
41 Hebbel's denigration of Stifter's abilities as a writer, to which many critics attribute the famous Preface to *Bunte Steine*, appeared in 1849 in the periodical *Europa*.
42 Walter 9.
43 Walter 12.
44 Paul Requadt, "Stifters *Bunte Steine* als Zeugnis der Revolution und als zyklisches Kunstwerk," *Adalbert Stifter: Studien und Interpretationen: Gedenkschrift zum 100. Todestage*, ed. Lothar Stiehm (Heidelberg: Lothar Stiehm Verlag, 1968) 150–154.
45 Helga Bleckwenn, "Adalbert Stifters *Bunte Steine*: Versuche zur Bestimmung der Stellung im Gesamtwerk," *Vierteljahresschrift des Adalbert Stifter Instituts des Landes Oberösterreich* 21 (1972): 105–117.

46 Martin Swales credits Stifter's generous and human response to the thematic impulse for "... a corresponding differentiation of narrative perspective that makes him a writer of real breadth and stature." See Swales *Novelle* p. 156.

Chapter II

"Granit"

THE TITLE OF THE FIRST work in Adalbert Stifter's collection of six novellas refers to a large, rectangular block of granite which sits conspicuously near the front entrance of the narrator's childhood home. The stone is described in the first paragraph of the story as having the "Gestalt eines sehr in die Lange gezogenen Würfels," with roughhewn sides and a top surface worn to a polished glaze by generations of the family having sat upon it. The continuing description immediately alerts the reader to the significance of tradition and familial continuity in the simple tale of a boy's folly and eventual redemption, with this social element coming to play an important part in the later depiction of the story's events and in the narration of a legend from the "Pestzeit," a story-within-a-story, as well.

For the purpose of analyzing and discussing the thematic complex of ego, initiative, and socialization in this particular work, the phenomenon of "family" will represent to a large extent the socialization component of the complex. The thematic elements of ego and initiative are diffused among several characters and character constellations. Different amounts of text are allotted by the author for the development of the thematic complex in the principal narrative (ca. 10 pages) and in the legend section (ca. 20 pages). This diffusion of the thematic interplay of ego, initiative, and socialization over two intermingled strands of the story represents a variation of the interplay which makes it seem at times uneven and understated; but this problematic exposition serves well as a starting point for the study of a thematic complex which varies in cogency and concentration among the three novellas considered in this study.

Already in the second paragraph of the story, the narrator's ego begins to be manifest. He introduces himself thus: "Eines der jüngsten Mitglieder unseres Hauses, welche auf dem Steine gesessen waren, war in meiner Knabenzeit ich" (17). But this brief, one-sentence introduction can be seen upon close scrutiny to contain the kernel of the total thematic complex of ego, initiative, and socialization which underlies the novella. In the quotation cited above the reference is to "meiner Knabenzeit" and "ich," but the individual is presented simultaneously as a "Mitglied unseres Hauses." All three elements in this latter term emphasize individual subordination to a larger social entity. The active element, the "initiative" of the tripartite thematic interplay is represented here quite simply by the verbal idea of "sitting." It serves as a connective between the two substantive elements of ego and socialization, with an implication of permissibility or possibility predicated upon the relationship of the former (the individual) to the latter (the social unit) .

The narrator's introduction of himself is then followed in the same paragraph by some seven statements of individual initiative, but all seven instances are coupled structurally with one or more clauses or phrases which refer to natural or impersonal phenomena. The result is a deemphasis of individual initiative or an integration of it into a broader thematic concern. The passage is quoted here, with the key words and figures expressing individualized initiative italicized and those which de-emphasize or qualify it in boldface:

Ich saß gerne auf dem Steine, weil **man** wenigstens dazumal **eine große Umsicht von demselben hatte**. Jetzt **ist sie etwas verbaut worden**. *Ich saß* gerne im **ersten Frühlinge** dort, wenn die **ersten milder werdenden Sonnenstrahlen** die **erste Wärme** an der Wand des Hauses **erzeugten**. *Ich sah* auf die **geackerten** aber noch nicht **bebauten Felder** hinaus, *ich sah* dort manchmal ein Glas wie einen weißen **feurigen Funken schimmern** und **glänzen**, oder *ich sah* einen **Geier vorüber fliegen**, oder *ich sah* auf den fernen bläulichen Wald, der mit seinen **Zacken an dem Himmel dahin geht**, an dem die **Gewitter und Wolkenbrüche hinabziehen**, und der so hoch ist, daß *ich meinte*, wenn **man auf den höchsten Baum** desselben **hinauf steige**, mußte **man den Himmel angreifen können**. Zu andern Zeiten *sah ich* auf der **Straße**, die nahe an dem Hause **vorübergeht**, bald einen **Erntewagen** bald eine **Herde** bald einen **Hausierer vorüber ziehen**. (17–18)

If one compares the italicized items above with those that are boldfaced, several things become apparent. First, one notices the difference in sheer bulk, with the non-ego centered elements in heavy preponderance. Secondly, one notes the degree of energy or the scope expressed by many of these natural or impersonalized images, which make the simple "ich saß" or "ich sah" of their ego-centered counterparts seem quite weak by comparison. Thirdly, the author's use of certain words and grammatical modalities in certain contexts can be observed: the frequent use of the impersonal "man" and the use of the passive with "werden." The words "Erntewagen," "Herde," and "Hausierer" ["peddler"] besides displaying assonant and alliterative compatibility can be seen as expressions of socially based phenomena. The use of the subjunctive to express belief or opinion is not in and of itself unusual. But its isolated use in this passage serves the related purposes of accurately expressing a child's delusion and, in conjunction with the other structural and stylistic points already mentioned, of creating a thematic atmosphere within which every depiction of ego-initiated action, no matter how mundane or trivial, has the potential for conflict with its immediate social context.

It could be argued that detailed analytical techniques are more applicable to the more concentrated forms of poetry or the short story, where there is less danger of overstating the significance of small structural elements such as clauses, phrases, and single words or verbal forms. This carefully created atmosphere, however, seems to be an integral part of Stifter's artistic vision and style. It will be seen, moreover, that the thematic interplay of ego, initiative, and socialization which is present in this structural and stylistic device of an atmospheric preface to the main narrative is also found in the strictly narrative portions of the work.

Since the use of structural relationships and details which help develop a thematic interplay is apparently consistent and frequent feature of Stifter's style throughout *Bunte Steine*, this chapter will concentrate henceforth more on an analysis of broader applications of that usage such as characterization, actional sequences, and structural manipulation and juxtaposition of paragraphs, passages, and larger narrative units. Detailed points of grammar and word selection may be cited again, however, wherever they seem particularly supportive for the interpretive thesis of this book.

The introductory or atmosphere-engendering passage at the beginning of "Granit" ends with the third paragraph (18), which is shorter than the first two and functions as a summation and reiteration of the ego, initiative, and socialization interplay already subtly outlined. The narrator's ego is nullified here in that he is asleep or beginning to drowse as youthful household members (and, hence, representatives of the social order) gather informally and sing lovely songs in the dark night ["anmutige Lieder in die finstere Nacht"]. Compared with the amount of text devoted to the creation of an atmosphere in some of the other novellas of *Bunte Steine*, these scant three paragraphs represent a high degree of stylistic concentration. In the admittedly brief mention of the grandfather in this third, summary paragraph, there is not only a foreshadowing of his role as mediator in the later action but also an implicit certification of his thematic role as an ego in proper relation to its social reality. This "rightness" will become manifest in the product of his initiative: kindly thought and action.

The thematic significance of the grandfather prefigured here is supported structurally by the introduction in the immediately following paragraph of a character who will become the thematic antipode of the kindly patriarch in the socialization interplay: "der Pechmann." This "grease peddler" is described immediately by the youthful narrator as a strange character ["ein Mann von seltsamer Art"] (18). The ambiguity conveyed by these words is further heightened in following lines by a description of the man's clothing, which has taken on the dusky hue of his ware over the years. His hand-pushed cart and grease containers are also glistening black in color. These concisely stated details convey in an understated fashion the negative attributes which can accrue to the individual ego in the pursuit of a solitary initiative. But Stifter's artistry here does not degenerate into a one-dimensional symbolism. The humanity of the peddler is preserved when he is further described in this same paragraph as having friendly eyes and the yellow-white hair of the elderly but hard-working poor of the region (18).

The thematic interplay of ego, initiative, and socialization is also present in the last part of this paragraph. The inhabitants of the neighborhood come forward to make their purchases of axle grease, and the methodical activity of the peddler then takes on a socialized aspect which contrasts noticeably with the ego-centered initiative of the boy. His fascination with this "personality" prompts him to be the first one there ["gewiss eher auf dem Platze als alle andere"] (19), whenever the peddler's cry is heard. Stifter inverts the time sequence by describing first the peddler's isolated "clean-up" activities after the crowd has left, and then by the chronologically precedent arrival of the boy. This is another structural means of narrowing the thematic focus gradually to ego-initiated activities and, by logical extension, to their consequences.

The tension only incipient in the last passage described above begins to build quickly in the succeeding paragraph. It reaches a climax with the first use of a direct quotation in the text when the peddler asks, "Willst du die Füße eingeschmiert haben?" (19). In this paragraph, which parallels in many aspects the one before it, there is again a balance of images to create at first only an intimation of ambiguous egocentrism. People in general are described as being in a gay but also mischievous ["schelmisch"] mood due to the spring sunshine. The mood is ascribed to everyone ["alle Menschen"], thereby softening by diffusion the negative connations of "schelmisch." The peddler's initiative in approaching the village and crying his wares is given a social turn, as in the preceding paragraph, by the immediate arrival of his customers; and once again it is isolated by the departure of the crowd and aligned structurally (and this time chronologically as well) with the action of the boy, who watches his clean-up activities closely. The narrator's description of himself at this juncture as sitting on the granite stone wearing trousers which he has outgrown provides an image of an individual personality which has reached a transitional stage. As was stated above, the tension implicit in this situation is climaxed in the sudden query of the peddler. The use of direct quotation seems a conscious artistic choice by Stifter which, besides adding some stylistic variety and animation to the narrative, also conveys an element of personalization. This personalization in turn posits thematically, in the context of the query, a potential collusion between two egos in a clearly irregular enterprise. Hence, a passage consisting of two rather short paragraphs whose respective internal structures are noticeably similar has brought the protagonist of the piece, the narrator in his boyhood, to the point of a decision: to act or not to act; to choose or not to choose.

The rationale for the decision clearly revolves around a blatant appeal to the ego. The boy himself admits in the next paragraph that he is honored to be addressed by such a prominent curiosity ["Merkwürdigkeit"] as the peddler. He readily seizes the initiative and holds his feet up for "greasing." Our impression of the egocentrism of his action is enhanced by the sensory image of the amber substance with its pleasant aroma, spreading almost of its own volition around the edges of the boy's soles. It is as though he experiences an authentic but nonetheless highly egocentric communion with a material substance as a result of his action. But the rapid departure of the peddler, leaving him alone again, and perhaps a growing intuition of the significance of being thus "stained" have left the boy with "ein zwar halb angenehmes aber deßungeachtet auch nicht ganz beruhigtes Gefühl" (20). Stifter extends the tension of the situation by having the narrator-protagonist embark immediately upon another episode of ego-initiated folly, this time with physically painful results. Motivated no doubt in part by a vague feeling of malaise as cited above, and also by the still active thrill of having initiated a situation which seems to have a great potential for his personal aggrandizement, the boy seeks out his mother to be first witness to his deed. The line-by-line balance of images continues here with the boy's too short trousers, a symbol of bourgeoning individuality, mentioned again and paired structurally with a comment on the social significance of Saturday. While the mischievous peddler is reintegrated into the communal scheme of things by virtue of waiting over for Sunday church, the youthful protagonist in this pivotal passage is left high but, unfortunately, not dry.

Given his duality of motivation, it is perhaps natural that the boy seeks approval from the figure that would represent for him a bridge between the personal and familial aspects of his own identity: his mother. But the picture of the boy's blithe but disastrous entrance into the dwelling as he leaves behind him step-by-step the pitchy manifestations of his ego, coupled with the picture of his mother sitting engaged in the service-directed activity of sewing precludes any chance of resolution of the thematic tension at this point. In fact, the negativity of his ego-centered initiative is climactically mirrored in the mother's violent outburst of anger and the strenuous thrashing she soon administers to the boy. And the author once again punctuates a thematically critical moment with a direct quotation, only the second in the narrative:

> Da sie mich so kommen und vorwärts schreiten sah, sprang sie auf. Sie blieb einen Augenblick in der Schwebe, entweder weil sie mich so bewunderte, oder weil sie sich nach einem Werkzeuge umsah, mich zu empfangen. Endlich aber rief sie: "Was hat denn dieser heillose eingefleischte Sohn heute für Dinge an sich?" (20)

In the paragraph immediately following, the image of initiative-run-rampant is completed. The mother, disregarding the boy's terror and the bespattering of her own clothing, the cobblestones and the other parts of the porch, flails away at his dirty feet with a switch that he himself has previously left outside because of a standing house rule. This last descriptive detail also seems to indicate that even legitimately socialized patterns of behavior can be compromised or distorted, if excessive tension caused by an ego-centered initiative elicits an even more radical action in response. An awareness of this aspect of his transgression is clearly expressed by the narrator in the next paragraph, when he states, "Ich war . . . weil ich mit meiner teuersten Verwandten dieser Erde in dieser Zerwürfnis geraten war, gleichsam vernichtet" (21). The next appearance of the mother a few lines later in the paragraph shows her in counsel with a domestic helper planning the necessary clean-up—an instant return to the sphere of collective, service directed activity. This thematic reintegration of the mother highlights once again the solitary dilemma of the boy, who instinctively seeks penitential refuge on a large stone in the corner of the entryway, which is used for the preparation of rough yarn for household use.

The mention of this second stone block seems to be at first a somewhat clumsy attempt at developing a motif. The similarity of this stone with the "Granit" of the title and introductory passage takes on deeper significance, however, when viewed as a unity which symbolizes not only the coherence of the social aspect of the thematic interplay, but which also reflects the unified nature of Stifter's conception for the total work .

To summarize at this point, it can be proposed that thematic elements of ego, initiative, and socialization have been developed structurally, stylistically, and contextually in the first five pages of the novella to the point of a climactic conflict and partial, albeit negative resolution. The understated but rich accumulation of images, symbols, and actions in these few lines to flesh-out and keep this thematic interplay of ego, initiative, and socialization solidly in the narrative foreground encapsulates both Stifter's artistic virtuosity and his apparent concern with those themes.

In the next section of the work, "Granit" exhibits thematic foci and narrative techniques which will later provide points of reference for comparing and contrasting it with the two other selections from *Bunte Steine* considered in this study. The most noticeable of these features are bound up with the preponderant significance of the thematic element of socialization in the latter thirty pages of "Granit." Structurally this is evident in the interpolation of lengthy passages describing a day-length hike through the region where the story is set, with narrations of historical and legendary events which have bearing on the concept of socialized versus ego-centered initiative; only in the final few pages of the story is there a return to the familial "Hof" where the story began. It is also noticeable that the majority of references in this part of the work to the other two elements of the thematic interplay, ego and initiative, are embodied in parable-like illustrations taken from the interpolated "tales," rather than from the main narrative itself (as was the case in the first half of the story). Hence, the youthful protagonist assimilates comparatively painlessly the precept of socially integrated behavior as being the only type really pertinent to the real present. The artistic danger presented by such a structural and stylistic imbalance in regard to the expression of a tripartite theme is avoided skillfully by Stifter's carefully constructed interim passage, consisting of some five pages wherein he reintroduces the figure of the grandfather.

Considered from the larger structural viewpoint, as to its relationship with the five pages of the novella which precede it, and to the section of nearly five times that length which follows it, the passage which depicts the initial interaction in the story between the boy and his grandfather can be viewed in two ways. The sequence of action in these paragraphs forms a clearly recognizable, logical conclusion to the action of the preceding passages. This sequential aspect of the passage is consciously expressed in what might be considered its penultimate paragraph, which consists solely of a step-by-step review of the foregoing events by the boy himself:

> Ich erzählte ihm nun, wie ich auf dem Steine gesessen sei, wie der Wagenschmiermann gekommen sei, wie er mich gefragt habe, ob ich meine Füße eingeschmiert haben wolle, wie ich sie ihm hingehalten, und wie er auf jeden einen Strich getan habe, wie ich in die Stube gegangen sei, um mich der Mutter zu zeigen, wie sie aufgesprungen sei, wie sie mich genommen, in das Vorhaus getragen, mich mit meinem eigenen Ruten gezüchtigt habe, und wie ich darnach auf dem Stein sitzen geblieben sei. (24–25)

Once again the stylistic choice of indirect reporting and its subjunctive modality seems to serve a dual purpose. The childlike nature of the narrator's perception of the described events is thus accurately expressed in this simplistic enumeration; but there is still a hint of ambiguity present here in this reiteration of a series of individual initiatives, an ambiguity which maintains the potential for thematic tension in these actions. A detailed analysis of this "grandfather" passage in its totality will in fact reveal a thematic as well as a strictly narrative integration with the total work. And, once again, this tight weave of structure, theme, and content is accomplished with unobtrusive artistic instinct.

The grandfather section serves not only as a structural denouement and thematic rounding-out of the narrative up to the point of its inclusion, but can also be seen as a second atmospheric preface which sets the stage for a further structural and narrative development in "Granit" of the thematic interplay of ego, initiative, and socialization .

The first lines of the grandfather section give an initial impression of this heretofore only alluded-to character, in terms as concentrated but also as thematically pregnant as those in the lines which introduced the youthful narrator on the beginning page of the novella: "In diesem Augenblicke ging der Großvater bei der hintern Tür, die zum Brunnen und auf die Gartenwiese führt, herein, und ging gegen mich hervor" (21). Significantly, it is the back door, with its semantic connotation of humility and its connections with the socially based phenomena of well and garden plot, which serves as the portal for the grandfather's active entrance into the story. This image of an ego totally integrated with its social context and role is immediately certified in the following lines, when he is described as an unfailing source of solace for the children of the household—ever anxious to help, but never one to place any blame. Stifter postpones here for some four pages the boy's answer to the old man's query as to the origins of his immediate state of discomfiture. The focus in the remainder of this paragraph is rather on the emotional response of the boy to this unfortunately belated encounter with what he intuits with childish acuity to be a proper role-model. The incoherent sobbing of the child as he attempts to explain the situation and particularly the holding up of his feet for the grandfather's inspection offer a pointed contrast to the earlier scene of eager compliance with the peddler's roguish suggestion. This is a rather touching picture of an innocent ego, but an ego nonetheless, shattered on the ruins of its own initiative. Even the previously admired golden brown of the pitch is now symbolically interspersed with angry red welts ["das häßliche Rot der Züchtigung"] (22).

The grandfather's response to this pathos is in keeping with his role as comforter and refuge, but stylistically he is allotted the third, and as far as the thematic interplay, probably the last pertinent instance of directly quoted discourse in the novella. He smiles and says: "So komme her zu mir, komme mit mir" (22). This quote seems to form a thematic whole with the two previously cited ones of the peddler and the mother, encompassing the interplay of ego, initiative, and socialization in generalized terms. And, indeed, the ensuing several paragraphs focus in the manner of a denouement on the matter-of-fact but still sympathetic ministrations of the old man as he skillfully cleans the boy's feet, changes his clothes, and helps him to regain his composure. Stylistically this tying-up of loose narrative ends is also expressed in the introductory phrasing of several of the paragraphs in this section. The idea of resolution is present in the expressions "Bei diesen Worten" and "Mit diesen Worten," which introduce the consolatory actions of the grandfather (22,23). But in their role as a thematic or atmospheric preface to the second major structural division of the work, containing the tale-within-a-tale, the grandfather passages show here the same balance of images as was evident in the opening passages. This balance keeps the thematic interplay of ego, initiative, and socialization in motion and serves structurally as a preparation for the more pointed narrative exposition or working-out of that thematic interplay in the pages that follow.

The boy is directed by the grandfather to leave the dwelling as unobtrusively as possible and to wait for him by the road. The old man also encourages the child at this point to accompany him on a journey on foot to a neighboring village. The possibility of a forthcoming lesson in socialization and integration of individual effort with a larger context is subtly introduced when the grandfather says, ". . . da wirst du mir erzählen, wie sich dein Unglück ereignet hat, und wie du in diese Wagenschmiere geraten bist" (23). This directive, coupled with the context of the boy being physically removed from his normal sphere of social interaction, the family farmstead, appears to gently impose upon him the posture of a student preparing for instruction in matters more philosophical than practical. This image is further developed in the following paragraph wherein the successful individual initiative of sneaking out of the courtyard undetected, in the course of which the boy significantly moves "sehr weit von dem großen Steine . . . weg," culminates in his watching from afar the efforts of two domestic helpers to eradicate the traces of his recent faux pas from the porch area. This sense of a more objectified consideration of the thematic interplay of ego, initiative, and socialization from the boy's viewpoint is skillfully and with subtle finality established in the last image of this paragraph:

> An der äußersten Grenze unserer Gasse sehr weit von der Haustür entfernt, wo der kleine Hügel, auf dem unser Haus steht, schon gegen die vorbeigehende Straße abzufallen beginnt, lagen einige ausgehauene Stämme, die zu einem Baue oder zu einem anderen ähnlichen Werke bestimmt waren. Auf diese setzte ich mich nieder, und wartete. (23)

The repetition of an imaging motif of the protagonist sitting upon a thematically significant object, poised on the brink of potential initiative is unmistakable. One need only remember the earlier depictions of the boy sitting on the granite block daydreaming and later in the same posture having his feet greased, and then of his sitting on the "yarn stone" in abject contrition.

At the same time, Stifter's artistry again prohibits an unnatural structural segmentation in the interest of a didactic exposition of his thematic interplay. Elements of the boy's potential egoism are carefully balanced in the following paragraphs (23-24) with the grandfather's service-oriented initiative and a gradual physical distancing from the site of the foregoing disruptions. As the two leave the house behind, they pass through the neighboring environs and out into the open countryside. This passage can be seen as an effective metaphor for a mental or spiritual progression from pre-occupation with an ego-initiated conflict, to an awareness of a broader social context, and on to an even more encompassing view of universal integration. Here the almost extirpated ego can, under the auspices of nature and a legitimate spiritual guide, begin to revive:

> Wir gingen auf dem schmalen Fußwege durch das Grün unsers Hügels auf die Straße hinab, und gingen auf der Straße fort, erst durch die Häuser der Nachbarn, auf denen die Leute uns grüßten, und dann ins Freie,hinaus .... Mein Schmerz und mein Kummer war schon beinahe verschwunden, ich wußte, daß ein guter Ausgang nicht fehlen konnte, da der Großvater sich der Sache annahm, und mich beschützte; die freie Luft und die scheinende Sonne übten einen beruhigenden Einfluß,... und Luft floß sanft durch meine Haare. (24)

The balance of ego, initiative, and socialization is continued in the following paragraph as the grandfather graphically reviews the physical damage caused by the boy's earlier misguided initiative, while at the same time assuring the boy that he is spared from further punishment and that his mother has approved his outing with the old man. The boy responds in his turn with the subdued, schematic account cited earlier of the crucial events.

At this point, Stifter's smooth implementation of narrative balance and juxtapositional subtlety notwithstanding, a transition both structural and thematic is perceptible. With the kindly inflected but unmistakably earnest declaration, "Du bist ein kleines Närrlein" (25), the old man serves indubitable notice that class is now in session. The second major structural division of the work begins, which involves an inculcation of the ethical tenets embodied by the thematic interplay of ego, initiative, and socialization, with the necessary supremacy of the latter, in the consciousness of the youthful narrator. This is achieved by the grandfather through a guided visual review (complete with periodic quizzes) of the surrounding geographic panorama from their vantage point atop the mountain ridge between their village of Oberplan and their destination of Melm, and also through the narration of events from the plague time which devastated the region during the time of the grandfather's grandfather. The first of these two procedures can be seen to serve the dual purpose of instilling a sense of community in the boy, as well as providing a general format for considering the interplay between that communal whole and the individual activities or initiatives which take place within it. The second component of the old man's tutelage, the narration-within-the-narration, provides a more detailed, dramatic format for developing instructive examples of this problematic relationship of ego to society—examples which can be more effectively related to and personalized by the young protagonist, especially in the actions and motivation of a pitch distiller's son.

At this point in the study of the thematic interplay of the elements of ego, initiative, and socialization in "Granit," consideration must be given to a couple of extensions or aspects of these elements which assume primary importance in this latter half of the work.

The concept of "ego" has been seen to manifest itself up to this point in the motivations and characterizations of the boy, the peddler, the mother, and the grandfather in pretty much that order. The egoism of the boy is depicted as a natural consequence of his youth and inexperience. That of the grandfather, at the other end of the elemental spectrum, is not divorceable from his socially integrated character. The egoism manifest in the actions of the peddler and the mother, however, seem somehow incongruent with the prevailing tone of natural and essentially positive, even if at times misguided personal endeavor in the rest of the work. And it is precisely these apparent incongruities that the grandfather feels called upon to elucidate at the beginning of his lengthy, on-going discourse with the boy about these matters of ego and society.

Labeling old Andreas, the grease peddler, as an "arger Schalk" ["mischievous scoundrel"] who has habitually delighted in such tomfoolery, the grandfather then takes some pains to extenuate the old rogue's behavior from the viewpoint of his having positive associations with the substance of grease, in that he makes his living from the sale of it (25). One has to wonder just how serious the old man is here, however, when he adds the supposedly supportive image of Andreas trudging about the countryside in all kinds of weather and sleeping in haystacks in order to follow his vocation. There is a definite feeling in these lines that the ironic allusion to physical hardship and semi-indigency contains the reverse of the values being posited here. This seems especially true in view of the final description of Andreas at the end of this section and quite near the end of the novella. There, the grandfather terminally delimits him as "nur ein Wagenschmiermann," ["just a wagon grease peddler"] capable of nothing but roaming the countryside with his black cask and greasing the feet of ignorant, foolish boys (51). The grandfather's extenuation of the mother's ego-initiated outburst seems much more logical and thematically straightforward. He claims for her the benefit of a misunderstanding as to her son's motivation in tracking grease through the house, and he assures the boy that it will all be cleared up to his eventual rehabilitation.

The thematically relevant point which appears to develop in this passage is that in the assessment of individual initiatives the degree of egoism involved, rather than its mere presence, is the chief ethical issue. This more complex view of the element of ego in its thematic interplay with initiative and socialization is narratively developed in the remainder of "Granit" primarily in terms of an apparent limitation by the author, of individual initiative to a very specific interrelatedness with social and often simultaneously with Christian values.

This latter religious aspect is in nowise overdone considering the epoch and milieu within which Stifter lived and worked, and about which he wrote. Allusions to the Faith are fairly frequent but not overstated throughout the entirety of *Bunte Steine*. This plain but unobtrusive religiosity, which usually appears somehow connected with nature imagery, is in fact the second extension of a thematic element mentioned above: the complication of the concept of socialization to include not only humanistic parameters but also an obligatory but imperfectly understood integration with a divinely ordered reality. The boy is promised that by the end of the grandfather's tale, he will comprehend "welche wunderbare Schicksale die Menschen auf der Welt des Lieben Gottes haben können" (25). At any rate, although this broader aspect of the meaning of the social element cannot be totally relegated to background or "color" status, it is the aforementioned complication of the concept of ego and its concomitant relationship to socialization in terms of the success or failure of individual initiatives, that will be the chief focus in this study.[1] The amount of narrative space and detail devoted to limiting individual initiative, based on the degree of egoism evident within each respective instance of it, will serve as one point of reference for comparing and contrasting "Granit" and the two other works from *Bunte Steine* selected for analysis in this book.

When the grandfather begins his attempt to develop the young narrator's social awareness, he points out several natural features of the landscape through which they are hiking (26). He identifies and explains the "Behringer Brünnlein," which serves people near and far with the medicinal properties of its limpid waters, and the gigantic pines which are apportioned among the citizens of Oberplan on the basis of the amount of taxes they pay. It is impossible to mistake the social connection here, and it isn't surprising that the boy instantly senses the form that the afternoon's outing with his grandfather is to take. When the old man asks if he can identify a distantly visible forested ridge, the boy immediately gives its topographical designation. He also gives its commercial or communal function, as if the two formed a single entity: "... das ist die Alpe, auf welcher sich im Sommer eine Viehherde befindet, die im Herbste wieder herabgetrieben wird" (27). The passage continues with more questions by the grandfather and topographical identifications by the boy. But the old man soon shifts his attention to a more specific and, as will be seen, even more thematically suggestive feature of the landscape—the numerous "Rauchsäulen" or smoke columns arising from the wooded panorama all about them.

Stylistically, the one-by-one identification of these apparently quite similar columns of smoke almost comes to verge on the tedious, especially when they are enumerated in the repeated context of their localities which were likewise listed a few paragraphs earlier. But Stifter stops just short of erring here, as the grandfather's blanket explanation seems to point up the relation of this seemingly naively structured, almost naturalistic passage to the thematic interplay of ego, initiative, and socialization. He says, "... diese Rauchsäulen kommen alle von den Menschen, die in dem Walde ihre Geschäfte treiben" (28). He proceeds to describe these various activities or initiatives in the natural sequence in which they occur: first come the timber cutters who clear the land; then the charcoal makers, whose ware is exported to distant locales; next come the hay makers, followed by the herb gatherers and finally the "Pechbrenner" or pitch distillers. These last, of which the old rascal Andreas is a traveling affiliate, are significantly the only group mentioned here as establishing dwellings even though they as well as the other woodland entrepreneurs "haben keine bleibende Stätte in dem Walde; denn sie gehen bald hierhin, bald dorthin..." (29). It could possibly be that distilling takes longer than some of the other enterprises mentioned, but there seems to be a conscious accentuation of the potential for egocentrism present in this paradoxical image of hut builders who are nonetheless constantly on the move. It is as if their life style imposes upon them a superficial, materialistic concept of social interaction with consequences for their character as exemplified by old Andreas.

In these same lines, an image with an almost uncanny double significance is evoked when the grandfather describes the smoke columns as having like their human creators, "keine bleibende Stelle, und heute siehst du sie hier und ein anderes Mal an einem anderen Platze" (29). The metaphorical duplication of the thematic interplay is fairly clear: there exists a tenuous kind of relationship between initiatives which are by nature isolated but whose by-products are material links with larger society. The other function of this image of wandering smoke columns is the unstated but still somehow plastic contrast of them with the pitch-stained footprints of the boy from the earlier part of the story. Here the pale unsettled manifestations of initiative are granted quiet legitimacy, reevoking in retrospect the total unacceptability of the more boldly evident and hence more egocentric initiative of the boy's action. One again senses Stifter's instinct for hermetic composition, with such related images going to form the "mineral bonds" which seal the strata of structure and narration and form the substance which is "Granit."

At this point in the story, the grandfather directs the boy's attention to settlements, buildings, and other human enclaves visible within the natural panorama they have already discussed. This procedure is pedagogically logical, but it also expresses with a gradually narrowing structural focus the author's ever-present concern with the interrelationships among human personalities, their actions, and their social contexts. After eliciting the various place names from the boy and supplying the names of many which are not visible from their observation point, the grandfather offers an explanation of his motives for this geography and social studies lesson:

> Da wirst du einsehen, daß in diesen Ortschaften viel Leben ist, daß dort viele Menschen Tag und Nacht um ihren Lebensunterhalt sich abmühen, und die Freude genießen, die uns hienieden gegeben ist. Ich habe dir darum die Wälder gezeigt und die Ortschaften, weil sich in ihnen die Geschichte zugetragen hat, welche ich dir im Heraufgehen zu erzählen versprochen habe. Aber laß uns weiter gehen, daß wir bald unser Ziel erreichen, ich werde dir die Geschichte im Gehen erzählen. (30)

The grandfather's outright assertion that he will now begin the story-within-the-story marks a narrational turning point in the novella. This structural shift is accompanied by a stylistic one away from the dialogue of the previous passages, with its direct discourse and didactic tone, to a series of noticeably longer paragraphs of straight-forward narrative, most of which is expressed in the third person. But again what appears to be a structurally simplistic narrative transition is balanced with imagery which both maintains the thematic focus and also confirms that the seeming artistic naivete of expression fits the unpretentious character of the grandfather.

To begin with, the ideas of "Leben," "Lebensunterhalt," and "Freude" are grouped in the first sentence of the passage cited above. It is important that, for the first time, socialization as expressed in the word "Lebensunterhalt" is given an emotional value: happiness or joy. And it is also significant that this happiness has an immediate moral re-enforcement in that it is granted by divine will. Hence, while the ego component of the thematic interplay becomes more complex and problematic, socialization becomes more limited to a specific state of temporal grace which is reached by a careful attention to the proper limits of individual initiative. In the remainder of "Granit," these proper limits will become more and more clearly defined; they include not only the direction of the ego towards productive, service-oriented initiatives but also a conscious socialization for its own sake. The grandfather himself exemplifies the tripartite balance when he breaks off his self-initiated, albeit service-directed discourse at the end of this passage and admonishes the boy that they must hurry on to their goal, a neighboring village where some business matter apparently awaits him.

Almost at the halfway point of the novella, the second section of the grandfather's lesson to the boy in the ways of people, nature, and the world begins. In a single paragraph extending for almost three full pages, the old man outlines in broad strokes and powerful images the trials and hardships from the plague which ravaged Oberplan and all of the surrounding areas in the time of his own grandfather. The narrative connection with the specific expression of the themes of ego, initiative, and socialization as they apply to the young boy is maintained when Stifter sets the inception of the plague in the first bloom of spring. This is the time of year when humanity as well as nature should be poised on the brink of new activity after the lull of winter. But the depressing paradox in the images presented here of the dead and the dying interposed among the blossoms (30–31) presages an important new aspect of the thematic interplay heretofore only hinted at. The nature of this somber new complication begins to develop quickly, beginning with the statement that even those who were fortunate enough to survive the sickness did not experience a normal convalescence but lingered in a state of debility which made them unable to pursue their individual activities or initiatives. The idea of a divine punishment had often been considered when the Oberplaners discussed in the wintertime the plague's outbreak in distant regions, but such a thing seemed unthinkable to them later in their own travail. The irony of this viewpoint is undeniable when the grandfather describes the situation in simple but telling terms: "Niemand hatte geglaubt, daß sie in unsere Wälder herein kommen werde, weil nie etwas Fremdes zu uns herein kömmt bis sie kam" (31). The remainder of this passage shows that the otherwise positive element of socialization, if it becomes too insular, can become equivocal and can lose its legitimizing function within a still larger arena of social interaction. These larger spheres of society included for the Austrian Stifter the political unity of the Empire, but the connection plainly expressed in this passage is that with "der Welt des lieben Gottes."

And what are the consequences for a society that has become insular or, in a manner of speaking, collectively egocentric? The depiction of social disintegration in this passage is grimly concise. Significantly, the disease is said to have broken out first in the "Ratschlägerhäusern" or council halls, which symbolize the secular essence of the communal endeavor. The people of the area begin to flee to and from each other in terror. Many seek refuge in isolation only to find lonely deaths. Religious burial ceremonies are soon dispensed with as the number of corpses mounts. Mass graves are hastily improvised in the fields. Homesteads are depopulated and neglected livestock roam the region. Smoke columns, seen earlier in the novella as symbols of human initiative, are conspicuously absent from the skies. Family members regard each other with fear and loathing: "Die Kinder liebten ihre Eltern nicht mehr und die Eltern die Kinder nicht, man warf nur die Toten in die Grube, and ging davon" (31). This last image surely embodies the final ascendance of brute egoism in attitude and action. There is a glimmer of hope in the lines immediately following which present the altruistic scene of able-bodied men helping widows and orphans with the indispensable grain harvest. But the stark warning implicit in the foregoing catalogue of failed initiatives, both individual and communal, culminates with the description of the priest attempting to deliver a sermon to the tiny, sobbing remnant of his congregation. Other than these seven faithful, all the others have fallen to the disease, are nursing the afflicted, or have given in to the general mistrust of human contact. The author has the priest symbolically fail in his attempt at sermonizing and has him deliver a quiet mass instead, the most traditional and anonymous of church offices. The thematic statement here is apparently that even initiatives sanctified by a society can be swept away in a wave of egoism if that society is not consistently modeled on a more universal, if never fully realizable ideal of spiritual community.

The resolution of this dilemma where all relationships— individual, familial, and communal— are foundering comes in the following lines from the realm of religious myth. A farmer brings the priest the saving insight, given to him literally by a little bird, that the cure is to eat gentian and pimpernel. In keeping with the thematic extension of socialization to include a religious dimension, it is the priest who disseminates this life-saving directive to the populace, and the scourge withdraws as quickly as it came. The smoke columns return, but this time they represent the purification fires which eradicate the last vestiges of the disease. The church bells again ring out to signal the reconvocation of the faithful— the same bells that ring in the eve of the Sabbath for the two travelers of the outer narrative as they reflect on those long past events: " 'Siehe,' sagte der Großvater, . . . 'diese Zunge sagt uns beinahe mit vernehmlichen Worten, wie gut und wie glücklich und wie befriedigt wieder alles in dieser Gegend ist' " (33). In the next paragraph the grandfather and the boy doff their hats and pray, an example of ritualized individual initiative which no doubt is meant to protect the community against such a catastrophe as the old man has just described. He explains that he keeps the Sabbath by limiting his own activities to hikes about the region, but he alludes to the gradual degeneration of the ancient custom when he compares his wife's life-long respect for the "Feierabend" with the contemporary tendency among their neighbors to ignore it. He relates how they continue working in the fields and houses until well after the bells have rung. It is interesting to note in this context that the apparently service-oriented activity of their nearest neighbor, the weaver, is cited in an unfavorable light. These images of the comprehensive danger of too much complacency about the relationship of religion to ego, initiative, and socialization are completed by the grandfather's recollection at the end of this passage, of a son's dying wish on the battlefield to hear the bells of Oberplan once more. This harmonized set of bells was cast so that the bells were in tune with one another, and human initiative is expressed as being insufficient to recreate their harmony should one of them become cracked or damaged. The wounded son died far from home, and his death is symbolic of the compromise which war entails for the true and proper relationship of the individual and his society to one another.

Having thus instructed the boy in the larger philosophical implications of the interplay of ego, initiative, and socialization using at first broad illustrations from local history and then more individualized examples from his own immediate sphere, the old man continues in the next paragraph to steer the discourse gradually towards examples of behavior which will be even more relevant to his young protégé. Stifter brings the boy and along with him the reader back to the narrative present by having him slip on the short green meadow grass. Here the grandfather reasserts the pedagogical purpose of their combined activity (the hike) when he shows the boy how to get better footing and remarks, "Siehst du, alles muß man lernen, selbst das Gehen. Aber komme, reiche mir die Hand, ich werde dich führen . . ." (35). The encouragement here to constructive contact with a broader source of experience, to reach out, encapsulates the essence of a valid pedagogical enterprise. But, as is to be expected, the paragraphs which follow obviate any too-abrupt shift in content or structure which would impair the artistic flow of the narrative for the sake of a didactic consolidation of its themes. The historical exemplum is kept in focus when the grandfather identifies the "Drillingsföhre," the ancient tree from which the little bird sang his curative for the plague. This back- and-forth between images from the narrative present and the narrative past continues for the next several pages, with the primary thematic interest apparently involving a re-establishment of the dramatic balance between individual initiatives and the more secular and temporal aspects of socialization.

The alternation of the paragraphs and passages expressing this balance begins with the grandfather's statement that the Drillingsföhre is spared from cutting by common agreement (35). This standing symbol of the limits of allowable initiative in the interest of a sanctified social unity is replaced in the next paragraph by a similar object, the "Machtbuche" ["the beech tree of power"]. This hardy, somewhat stunted but densely foliated tree stands in isolation on the high ridge and is referred to by the grandfather as "der bedeutsamste Baum in der Gegend." This appellation seems somewhat surprising considering the immediately preceding exaltation of the other tree, but it is the practical function of the Machtbuche as an indicator of the seasons which lends it prestige among the local inhabitants. Significantly, the crown of this natural weathervane is described as being so thick that: "nicht ein einziges Äuglein des Himmels hindurch schauen kann" (35). This highly figurative expression signals the textual turn from the sacred back to the secular.

The chronological juxtaposition of outer and inner narratives continues throughout the remainder of the novella, but it seems particularly concentrated here. The grandfather asks the boy to keep a living memory of him after he is gone. Almost simultaneously the two see the village of Melm coming into view below them. The old man then recounts the anecdotes of a young dairymaid and a crippled miller, who managed to perform their respective tasks despite great difficulties during and immediately after the plague period. The old priest is listed in the same sentence as the defunct bathhouses as simply another individual agent whose functionality was sorely stressed. This refocusing on the practical, active aspect of human interaction is narratively supported in the next paragraph (37), by the arrival in Melm. There the boy mulls over his impressions of what he has heard and what he now witnesses in the courtyard of the farmer his grandfather has come to visit. There are wagons, plows, and harnesses, all stored in readiness for after the Sabbath, and the hired hands and maids go to and fro finishing their tasks before the holiday. This reviewing and blending of impressions seems to be the essential purpose of the paragraph. The thematic interplay of ego, initiative, and socialization is recalled as well, when the narrator says: ". . . und die Dinge gesellten sich zu denen, mit denen ohnehin mein Haupt angefüllt war, zu Drillingsföhren Toten und Sterbenden und singenden Vöglein."

When the grandfather finishes his business and he and the boy begin to retrace their journey homeward, the old man returns to his account of the plague. It is not at all surprising, considering the structural and imaginal pattern of thematic balance throughout "Granit," that the author returns in the next two passages to the concept of a religious versus a secular communality. The old man recounts the eventual consecration of the mass graves described earlier and the erection of the "Pestsäule," a column with a crucifix on top commemorating the catastrophe. Stifter also connects this paragraph with the thematic counterpoint which follows in the next through the figure of the tradition-conscious grandmother. The boy here credits his grandmother for having already told him of the plague column and this is followed by the old man's comments on the human flaw of forgetfulness, even on a community-wide scale (38). At this point a long passage of scenic description and nature imagery again sets the stage for the overtly didactic tone of the tale-within-a-tale. Pinpointing its location on the forested slopes in the distance, the old man describes a craggy height above a clear lake, which was the setting for the final part of his tale. Some of the thematically pertinent images and concepts of earlier passages are again repeated: the smoke columns, the barely socialized pitch distillers, and divine retribution. A distiller, in seeking to avoid the common travail which "Gott über die Menschen verhängt hatte," moves his family to seclusion on a high, wooded headland above a lake in the mountains. The fault of this endeavor, in terms of the religious aspect of socialization which Stifter has so carefully outlined in the preceding pages, is clearly expressed in the citation of God's intervention. But the thematic connection of the man's initiative, and those which emanate from it, with the temporal aspects of human society comes to assume increasing prominence throughout the remainder of the grandfather's tale. The distiller violently discourages all but minimal contact with his fellow beings, and this contact takes the form of the wandering grease peddlers who procure from him their stock. When he learns from them the plague has entered the general area, he flees not just to the limits of the sparsely inhabited terrain, but even further to where human activity has never encroached upon nature (42). As if to emphasize the radical nature of this self-imposed isolation still further a figure from an even earlier epoch is mentioned, a nobleman from the time of the Thirty Years War. This ancient figure was successful in the altruistic act of hiding his daughters at the mountain lake, safe from the conflagrations of war. But his castle, a symbol for his individual ego, is burned to ruins. Interspersed among these depictions are the boy's periodic assertions in the outer narrative that he recognizes in the distance the sites of these happenings, and that he has some familiarity with the ruins. These comments evince a growing competence as he progresses in his ethical apprenticeship.

There are some redeeming qualities in the action the distiller has taken in that he has removed his family to supposed safety, and the group is equipped with the implements and materials for agriculture, pitch distillation, and animal husbandry—all ostensibly socially productive activities. But here again, the immediate juxtaposition of an ambiguous situation maintains the thematic tension inherent for the author in all actions initiated by a single personality. The distiller's own brother, serving as an "alter ego," returns of his own volition to their former abode below, as if uneasy at this flight from all social connections. He does agree to signal the onset and progress of the plague with agreed upon sequences of smoke columns. The responsibility for this signal is to be passed on in the event of the brother's demise to a reliable third party, with the promise of a monetary reward after normalcy returns. The ambiguous nature of this act derives from the fact that the distiller expects others through family affiliation or monetary reward to work towards his welfare, while he intentionally cuts himself off from contact with them. It is hard to ignore the potential thematic implications of the long series of subjunctives in this passage. The one-sidedness or egocentrism of the arrangement seems to be pointed up by this stylistic feature and by the example of the three brothers which the grandfather cites at this point. According to local legend these three worked out a similar system of smoke signals but for mutual assistance and rescue. The refugees on the headland do, however, receive the signal that the plague has entered the immediate vicinity, and at this suspenseful juncture there is a brief return to the outer narrative. The old man interrupts his tale to button the boy's jacket and his own against the coolness of their evening hike back home. This simple, caring gesture in the context of a return to society also contrasts markedly with the elaborate but fatefully antisocial maneuverings of the distiller.

When the old man continues his story, the religious aspect of the distiller's doomed initiative is clearly evident in the description of it as a divine temptation ["eine Versuchung Gottes"] (43). But as religion in "Granit" is consistently bound up with the component of socialization in the thematic interplay, the consequences are depicted in collective terms, even though on a small, familial scale. The household members die off, leaving at last only the son of the distiller alive. The distiller, who himself initiated the flight to the headland, has had to bury the others, and he and his wife after witnessing the horribly ironic consequences of their withdrawal from social contact perish alone. They must remain unshriven and unburied because their son is too young to perform these final tasks. It is noticeable in the structure of this passage, which consists of a single paragraph extending for almost five pages, that a narrative concentration is intended. This concentration takes the form of a sequential cataloguing of the orphaned boy's initiatives to survive, to find his way home, and to care for a stricken girl he has discovered in a blackberry thicket. Bearing in mind the didactic purpose and intended target (the young protagonist of the outer narrative) of this exposition of successful, partly successful, and clearly failed individual initiatives, it is fitting that there again be a balance of the elements of ego and socialization connected with the various actions. The orphan boy cannot manage his parents' burial, but he is able to set free the livestock for their own survival. He is afraid of the corpses in the hut, but he has learned enough woods-lore in the context of his upbringing to survive on his own in the wild. It can be seen in these images that the boy's social or familial relationships have, in their degenerate form, put him in dire enough straits. But in their pre-catastrophe form they have given him training in skills suitable for the marginal and semi-social life-style of the pitch distillers. The now critical ability to make the connection with a larger social whole is, however, still suspensefully lacking. The boy symbolically repeats his parents' misguided attempt at escape by climbing even higher on the headland, away from the world below. He is seeking a vantage point from which to plan his descent, but this initiative fails nonetheless: "Er wußte nicht mehr wie sie in den Wald hinauf gekommen waren. Er ging auf die höchste Stelle des Berges, er kletterte auf einen Baum, und spähte, aber er sah nichts als Wald und lauter Wald" (44). His previously successful action of releasing the livestock has also become somewhat questionable because he cannot find them again. The thematic point here seems to be that survival is necessarily an ego-centered initiative which has validity in critical circumstances. But the degree of success to be expected from such ego-actuated activities is always limited, as seen in the boy's frustrations. Or, as in the case of the parents, there may be a complete failure to survive if this egocentrism becomes the collective viewpoint and replaces or impinges upon ethically based social relationships.

Not surprisingly, considering the thematic density of this passage, the opportunity for reestablishing a proper social context for the distiller's son begins to take shape almost immediately when he discovers an ailing girl. The boy instinctively intuits the preciousness of this new contact as evidenced by his wildly beating heart, and several pages follow which describe in detail how he cares for her. He did not flee from her, as he well could have, even though she was clearly infected by the same plague that drove their respective families into the wilderness. It is as if these two children represent a social microcosm which must find anew in the pristine world of nature the essential, love-engendered foundation of human society.[2] At the paragraph's end the grandfather in the outer narrative pauses only long enough to summarize the relevance of this example for his young charge before continuing his tale and the trek homeward. Then follows a description in simple but effective images of their descent to Oberplan—a symbol perhaps for an implicitly sanctioned movement towards a social context. This action is paralleled by the situation which now takes place in the inner narrative, as the grandfather continues his tale .

The two orphaned children likewise begin a descent back to civilization or, thematically speaking, to socialization. The boy is able in his new role as protector to subdue the impulse for individual action and to reason out, together with his companion, the right course to pursue. They decide to follow a nearby stream downward until they reach some human habitation, which is always to be found near running water. The boy's survival skills are again in the narrative foreground, but this time they are combined with the gentle care he shows towards the still enfeebled girl during the arduous trek down the mountain. This modification of a previously ego-centered initiative to a service oriented one is summed up in the ironic comment which follows immediately after a detailed account of his now altruistic actions: he beds down for the night "wie er sich in den ersten Tagen im Walde gebettet hatte" (49). The image here which blends his previously isolated initiative, fittingly expressed as a reflexive, with his new role of protector and provider links the character of the distiller's son with that of the grandfather who tells his story so many years later. And the example of this other boy who lays a foundation for meaningful integration of personal initiative and ethical or social duties is no doubt most impressive for the young grandson.

But Stifter, consistent with his approach throughout the novella, does not rely structurally on a single narrative or imaginal strand for support of his thematic exposition. Two thematically significant images bring this long paragraph to a conclusion: the descriptions of nature given in the course of the children's descent and a reference to the earlier pact between the distiller brothers. The trees and woodland creatures which have hitherto been depicted in general, usually ominous terms become increasingly individualized and friendly. Different species of foliage and fauna are depicted, as the children physically draw nearer and nearer to their hoped-for reabsorption into human society. Also, their legitimate exploitation, as now nascent social personalities, of natural resources, i.e. their eating of wild apples and cherries shortly before they reach cultivated fields, contrasts strikingly with the waste of these same fruits in the grandfather's earlier descriptions of the plague miseries. The paragraph ends with the elaborate but also failed initiative of the distiller's brother and his now meaningless smoke signals. This conclusion is necessitated by narrative and structural logic, no doubt. But it also exemplifies Stifter's techniques of reiterating motifs, symbols, and images throughout the course of "Granit" to keep the thematic interplay of ego, initiative, and socialization before the reader in very nearly every passage of the work.

This constant compaction of narrative material of similar structural, contextual, and thematic substance resembles the natural compositional process of the novella's geological symbol, granite. The process continues in the short paragraph which precedes the denouement of the grandfather's exemplary tale of the "Pechbrenner." As they finally regain the family farmstead, the grandfather tells the boy: "Da wir müde sind, und da es so warm ist, so setzen wir uns ein wenig auf den Stein, ich werde dir die Geschichte zu Ende erzählen" (50). This narratively logical situation implies a self-imposed suspension of their own hitherto successful action of hiking home. It also contains in the reference to the stone a symbol of tradition and socialization which can be traced back to the first lines of the novella. There appears at this juncture to be at last a structural opportunity for an outright assertion of the thematic significance of all that has gone before. Such a summation is offered symbolically in the following, narratively compact paragraph in which the orphaned children of the distiller's tale are reunited with their surviving relatives, grow to maturity, and come together again in marriage.

This seemingly straightforward resolution is, however, characteristically developed by another series of balanced images which would make any abrupt, didactic assertion of a thematic conclusion artistically incongruent at this point. The distiller's son and the little girl from the blackberry thicket are brought to his uncle, who has already returned to the headland and burned—in fear and probably disgust—not only the contaminated cabin but also the mouldering remains of his kinfolk. There is no mention of a possible later consecration of the remains, for the distillers live on the fringe of society. The girl is then removed by her own relatives from the uncle's combined dwelling and still, the site of perhaps necessary but still essentially egocentristic activity. A positive image of rehabilitation then follows, which balances the potentially negative connotations of the boy's return to the socially ambivalent position of a distiller: "Der Knabe blieb nun bei seinem Oheim in der Hütte, wurde dort größer und größer, und sie betrieben das Geschäft des Brennens von Wagenschmiere Terpentin und andern Dingen" (50). The resolution of the inner narrative finally does occur when the "blackberry girl" now grown-up and marriageable returns for her childhood rescuer. They ride off to live in her manor house, a dwelling representing the epitome of socially successful initiative, and the erstwhile son of a distiller rises to the opportunity. After guiding his individual activities into greater understanding and competence, he marries the girl and administers their estates to the satisfaction and admiration both of his social equals and of those who are economically dependent on him. The boy who had to learn on his own the proper interrelationship of ego, initiative, and socialization, sanctioned by a divine will manifest in nature, is now an example for the world (and particularly for the young narrator) to follow.

The understated style and fairy-tale tone of the final passage of the distiller's tale keep the thematic interplay suspended just long enough for it to be resolved in the more realistic outer narrative as well. Structurally, the length of the final section closely approximates and balances that of the novella's opening section. In these last few pages, however, there is no longer a structural, stylistic, and contextual juxtaposition of images, actions, and characters to create that tension between the elements of ego, initiative, and socialization. There is rather a compositional amalgam which consolidates those thematic elements into a final image of reconciliation and grace. After lingeriing for a while on the granite stone, the old man and boy are called to a late supper by the grandmother. The old lady at first chides her spouse for ruining a green, glazed basin earlier when he rescued the boy from his pitchy dilemma. But the tone of reconciliation in these last scenes is affectionately underscored by the grandfather, when he counters this possible limitation or negation of his earlier initiative. He not only asserts the priority of psychological reintegration (or resocialization) over the maintenance of external objects, but he also incorporates the initiative of the grandmother herself, this exemplar of successful secular and spiritual socialization, into this viewpoint:

> Der Großvater lächelte und sagte: " So zerbrechen wir die Schüssel, daß sie nicht einmal aus Unachtsamkeit doch genommen wird, und kaufen eine neue; es ist doch besser, als wenn der Schelm länger in der Angst geblieben wäre. Du nimmst dich ja auch um ihn an." Bei diesen Worten zeigte er gegen den Ofen, wo in einem kleinen Wännchen meine Pechhoschen eingeweicht waren. (52)

The grandfather is concerned with preventing some future mistake which might arise from the one which first led to the ruined basin. Although he clearly recognizes the phenomenon of individual needs in a critical situation, he continues to promote a natural consideration for the general good as a crucial aspect of individual initiative.

The traditional avenue for socialization of the ego and its initiatives has been shown in "Granit" to involve either service to those in need, as manifest in the actions of the grandfather himself and of the distiller's son, or to pursue one's occupation within cultural guidelines. The more these two approaches can be combined in the individual actions of its members, the more in keeping with the divinely ordered scheme of things will be the communal existence. The mother and father of the youthful narrator are briefly shown in both attitudes in the final paragraphs of the story, and this probably prefigures the success their son will achieve in his quest for social assimilation and personal fulfillment. The mother is away caring for a sick relative, but she returns to tuck-in the half-slumbering youth. The father is shown reading in bed, a habit which probably represents his role as family administrator and spiritual guide, but he responds as a loving parent to the boy's "good night." The last ego-related action of the boy is an unconscious one— a dream. In it the confused images of characters and events, both real and legendary, contemporary and ancient, swirl in a nightmare. But he awakens on Sunday morning ensconced in the security of rightly motivated activities, such as the holiday breakfast and preparations for church. His walk to the church is characterized by bright sunlight and the calm recognition of natural features which figured meaningfully in his dream, such as the mountain-ash tree cited by his grandfather in the previous evening's twilight as a symbol of the sombre enigma which nature represents for human kind. The boy's story ends with the scene of the family entering the church, where the father and grandfather have already taken their places in the "Bürgerstühlen"— icons of the thematic resolution.

Although from a thematic viewpoint the novella itself could also end here, Stifter maintains the artistic integrity of the work to the end. He comes full circle in the two brief final paragraphs, to the narrative present of the adult narrator— the time frame of the novella's first paragraph. The symbol of the stone also recurs, with a new generation now playing about it. And just as the very first paragraph contained only an intimation of the tension between ego, initiative, and socialization, the final two paragraphs embody a muted echo of its resolution. The mother, aged now, gazes from her granite resting place out into the vista of the surrounding landscape, thinking of the sons she has raised and sent forth into the wide world. The narrator says he clearly recalls the grandfather's tale, especially the beautiful foundling girl, "aber von den Pechspuren, die alles einleiteten, weiß ich nichts mehr..."(54).

A good case can be made, then, for the interplay of ego, initiative, and socialization as a dominant thematic strain in Adalbert Stifter's novella "Granit." The structural juxtaposition of sections, passages, paragraphs, and even single lines; the stylistic choice of narrative and grammatical modes and individual words; the textual balance, duplication, and recapitulation of images, actions, symbols, and characterizations—all of these compositional elements contribute to the presentation of this interplay and the resolution of the tensions arising from it.

Yet if one abstracts analytically from this artistic whole the single component of theme, there is an unmistakable quality of diffuseness in it. The thematic interplay of ego, initiative, and socialization can be viewed artistically as a dynamic unity, but the single elements themselves are noticeably dispersed and diversified in "Granit." The concept of "ego" must include the innocent, the equivocal, and the integrated varieties. The concept of "socialization" must include the familial as well as the communal, and even spiritual and natural possibilities. The depiction of initiatives runs the gamut from actions which are childishly egocentric or overtly malicious, through the socially tolerable and survival necessitated, to the universally applauded and religiously ritualized. This thematic diffuseness is, of course, bound up with the "frame" structure of the multiple time and narration levels, and the autobiographical sources of the content must be considered as largely determinant of the artistic form as well. As I. E. Walter reaffirms in his "Hinweise" to the Bergland edition of *Bunte Steine*, it is none other than the "Stifterbertelchen" himself who hikes over the hills with his grandfather here.[3] In the following chapters of this study, Stifter's continued use of thematic and compositional diffusion or his movement away from it will provide one basis for contrast and comparison among "Granit" and the two other novellas selected from *Bunte Steine*. Granite is a wonderfully solid material, but it is not the "marble" of unchanging classical form.

NOTES

1. Sagara designates Stifter's overall literary treatment of religion as a non-participatory nostalgia, 229.
2. Konrad Steffen likewise perceives this youthful union as the beginning of "eine neue Gesittung, eine neue Kultur," 143.
3. Walter 9.

Chapter III

"Kalkstein"

THE COMPOSITIONAL PRINCIPLE of "Granit," the first novella in Stifter's *Bunte Steine*, could be described as one of compacted diffusion, that is, the reiteration of structural, stylistic, and thematic elements within differentiated time frames, plot lines, and character complexes to achieve an integrated artistic whole. The general compositional approach of "Kalkstein," the second work in the collection, might be seen then as the reverse process: a kind of sublimated concentration. There is in this simple story of the life and death of an eccentric provincial pastor only one dominant character, the pastor himself, and there is little narrative action which does not center on this character. There are, it is true, several distinct shifts of time frame and narrative viewpoint in "Kalkstein," including an authentic story-within-a-story. But these are also focused squarely on the character of the protagonist and are not structural paths to a true narrative diffusion, as was the case in "Granit." The story-within-a-story, for example, is a factual reminiscence in the first person by the main character, and not a parabolic exemplar involving a second set of characters. Since the position of this study is to view "Kalkstein" as part of a collection which shares a pervasive thematic bond, the initial impetus for such narrational variation can be assumed to be ideational. The following textual analysis will seek to demonstrate that Stifter's general compositional approach in "Kalkstein" is a simultaneous depiction of a concentrated personality or ego (which because of notable eccentricities appears to be in dubious balance with its social milieu) and a narrative sublimation of that ego to extract the reasons behind its problematic profile. In keeping with the common thematic interplay, these reasons are in large part revealed by the limitations of the protagonist's initiatives, but it is the variation of that interplay that calls forth the structural and stylistic peculiarities which distinguish "Kalkstein" from its antecedent in the collection.

The author begins in the novella's first paragraph to develop this simultaneous depiction and analysis of his main character. In addition, he sets a general narrative tone and thematic emphasis which will continue throughout the work. The very first line of the story is this declaration by the author: "Ich erzähle hier eine Geschichte, die uns einmal ein Freund erzählt hat, in der nichts Ungewöhnliches vorkommt, und die ich doch nicht habe vergessen können" (54). This description, although meant perhaps in part ironically (see Stifter's "Vorrede" [5–12] for his professed views on the artistic significance of the apparently mundane), emphasizes the importance of the ideas or psychological content of the tale over the narrative action or plot. The rest of the introductory paragraph supports this claim of ideational supremacy. The occasion for the narration is said to have been a philosophical debate among a company of friends as to the nature and origin of what they refer to as "Geistesgaben." Although this term is somewhat difflcult to render in translation, it involves positive capacities of the spirit and mind. In their discussion of the gifted individual, the company designates these phenomena as both a faculty ["Vermögen"] and abilities ["Fähigkeiten"], terms which strongly suggest the thematic aspects of ego and initiative. In fact if one looks back to the second line of the paragraph, there is a simply stated prefiguration of the entire thematic interplay of ego, initiative, and socialization: "Unter zehn Zuhörern werden neun dem Mann, der in der Geschichte vorkommt, tadeln, der zehnte wird oft an ihn denken" (54). It is evident that there is to be a social and judgmental aspect to the following depiction of a unique ego and its actions. But the same lines also indicate the problematic nature of this judgment when seen from a majority viewpoint. Thus, one begins to see in this first paragraph of "Kalkstein" a prefatory passage analogous in several technical respects to the opening passages of "Granit." There is once again a general encapsulation of the dominant thematic complex of ego, initiative, and socialization. There is also the same balance of images, structural arrangement, and even stylistic choices to foreshadow narrative suspense: the story is commonplace yet unforgettable; many will fault the protagonist, but some will reflect deeply upon him; the opinions on "Geistesgaben" are diverse, yet the claim for divine ordination comes significantly last. There is a structural and stylistic distancing from the material, as expressed by the use of the subjunctive voice in the friends' debate and by the permanent shift in narrative viewpoint at the paragraph's end to that of the second narrator. Yet this distancing has been counterbalanced by subjective images of interest and concern on the part of the first narrator. The differences between the "psychological preface" here and the atmospheric one at the beginning of "Granit" are, however, just as obvious as the similarities. The images and thematic relationships in the opening passages here are all expressed in terms of either intuitive perceptions or theoretical concepts. There are, with the single exception of a brief allusion to the painter Raphael, no specific people or concrete objects in the first paragraph. Yet, the final result is not a narrative devitalization but rather an effective preparation for considering the more problematic variation of the thematic interplay of ego, initiative, and socialization which is presented in "Kalkstein."

"Kalkstein" is, in short, more "artificial" than "Granit," and as such it is more effectively realized along straightforward narrative lines. The forward momentum of the story's action is developed by means of a consistent structural and contextual pairing of the main character, the eccentric pastor, with a contrastive but sympathetic secondary character. This pairing technique, which provides the narrative format for presenting and simultaneously analyzing the pastor's ego, initiatives, and social interactions, is prefigured in the first paragraph by the pastor's connection with the theoretical tenth person who will supposedly reflect upon him and also with the first narrator, who cannot forget his story. With the beginning of the second paragraph, the coalescence of characterization and explication involving both the pastor and those characters which are in contrast to him begins to assume narrative and structural preeminence in the work.

The narrative viewpoint in "Kalkstein" shifts in the second paragraph from the "ich" of the author/narrator to the "ich" of his friend, a traveling government surveyor. This new viewpoint is maintained for the remainder of the novella, with the exception of the structurally and thematically integrated interpolation near the center of the work of a lengthy autobiographical passage written from the viewpoint of the pastor himself. There is never further mention of any of the other characters referred to in the prefatory passage, notably the original narrator. Nor is there any real attempt at a fluidity of structural transition here, as the paragraph begins simply with the statement, "Da erzählte mein Freund seine Geschichte" (55). The first paragraph remains, then, an apparent introduction into the particular variation of the ego-initiative-socialization interplay which forms the thematic foundation of the novella. The second paragraph, by contrast, begins immediately with a delineation of the two characters who will soon become the focus of the story: the surveyor and the poor pastor.

As the surveyor is the first of the pair to be described, and because throughout the work Stifter allots to him nearly as much space and exposure as to the pastor, there is some justification for interpreting his character as a sort of opposite number with equal significance for the thematic exposition manifest in the narrative. But the underlying preeminence of the pastor's character for "Kalkstein" is evident by the end of the second paragraph, which reveals what the major function of the surveyor/narrator will be. The surveyor will serve as witness, confidant, and reporter in the ongoing analysis of the poor pastor. In fact, the structural balance between the two characterizations seems intended to strengthen the narrative focus on the personality and quirks of the pastor in contrast to the unerring normalcy of the surveyor.

The second paragraph begins with a detailed but concise self-description by the surveyor, from which the image of an active, socially integrated personality emerges—an image which does not change to any appreciable degree throughout the rest of the story. It is also interesting from a stylistic perspective that, although the passage begins with what appears to be a direct quote, there are no quotation marks present in the text. This may have been an oversight on the part of the original publisher or perhaps on the part of the author himself. But given Stifter's proclivity for nonstandard spelling and punctuation, one might assume that this is a deliberate stylistic underscoring of the subordination in characterization of both the first and second narrators, regardless of their textual presence, to the protagonist:

> Ihr wißt alle, sagte er, daß ich mich schon seit vielen Jahren mit der Meßkunst beschäftige, daß ich mit Aufträgen dieser Art von der Regierung bald hierhin bald dorthin gesendet wurde. Da habe ich verschiedene Landesteile und verschiedene Menschen kennen gelernt . . . Da kam ich öfter in das nahe gelegene Dorf Schauendorf, und lernte dessen Pfarrer kennen, einen vortrefflichen Mann, der die Obstbaumzucht eingeführt, und gemacht hatte, daß das Dorf, das früher mit Hecken, Dickicht und Geniste umgeben war, jetzt einem Garten glich, und in einer Fülle freundlicher Obstbäume da lag. (55)

Besides establishing that the narrator's character is nonproblematic, this section of text goes on to provide in its presentation and analysis of the character, actions, and subtly ambiguous social significance of the main character, "der arme Pfarrer im Steinkar," some imaginal and structural connections with the soon-to-be-introduced main narrative line of the story. Some of the connections are observable by the end of this same paragraph, some of them extend into the immediately succeeding passages, and still others project into much later narrative sections, where they serve to recapitulate a thematic contrast. This technique is reminiscent to some extent of the reiterative and alternating principles in "Granit," but here the structural movement seems always to be linear rather than circular, and it moves toward an ever greater refinement and psychological subtilization of the thematic interplay, rather than toward a resolution of the problems presented.

At any rate, the narrator/surveyor is pictured in his own words as a civil servant whose personal initiatives revolve around service to his society and gregarious interaction with people in many different parts of the land. This image would in itself provide sufficient contrast for the subsequent pairing of his balanced personality with the eccentric character of the pastor. But Stifter's intent to isolate and analyze the psychology of his protagonist as an example of a perhaps unresolvably problematical interplay of the elements of ego, initiative, and socialization is also augmented here by a brief but significant narrative detail; he momentarily pairs the narrator with another pastor, whose integration of self and society is shown in the passage quoted above to be perhaps even more happily and productively resolved than that of the surveyor. The single depiction of this well-rounded orchardman and cleric, coming as it does in the same paragraph as the initial appearance of the protagonist, serves an additional function beyond providing the simple thematic contrast of a successful life within a social context. The fact that the orchardman, too, is a member of the spiritual order resolves early the question of whether there is to be any equivocation in the analysis of the protagonist's dilemma, on the basis of a theological mystique. There is indeed a significance to the ecclesiastical status of the protagonist in "Kalkstein," but by describing the contrastive productivity of the orchardman, Stifter indicates that ordination does not guarantee a homogeneous attitude towards social integration.[1]

The second priest, the protagonist, appears in the story only a few lines after the description of the orchardman and is immediately depicted in terms of his threadbare attire and inhibited social comportment. To be openly critical of a man of the cloth, even in fiction, would have been almost unthinkable to a writer of Stifter's time, place, and psychology. It is not surprising then that the focus of the story is not upon the possibility of a priest's failed initiative, but rather upon the problematical nature any human endeavor may manifest, regardless of external social sanction or ritualization. At this stage the presentation and probing of the poor pastor's character is only beginning, but the general direction toward evaluative complexity is clear by the paragraph's end and does not change significantly until the tale's final passage.

The character of the surveyor is introduced in broad outline. We then see him approach the site of a banquet given by his friend, the orchardman, at the latter's parsonage in the village of Schauendorf. The surveyor descends from the higher lying fields, passes through rows of fruit trees and enters the parsonage grounds. There he witnesses through an open window the bustle of preparation and service which accompanies such gatherings. He is drawn without ceremony into the hall and conviviality by the orchardman, who seats his guest at his reserved place and encourages him with relaxed cordiality to introduce himself during the feast to anyone he does not already know. The surveyor is fully integrated into the festivities by the midpoint of the paragraph, when he declares, "Ich wurde mit manchen Anwesenden bekannt, von manchem erfuhr ich Namen und Verhältnisse, und da die Gerichte sich ablöseten, und der Wein die Zungen öffnete, war manche junge Bekanntschaft schon wie eine alte" (56). The choice of the phrase "Namen und Verhältnisse" ["Names and relationships"] in this passage seems to imply a conscious if casual social intercourse, and the banquet can be viewed thematically as a symbol for the socialization process in schematic form. It is also thematically significant that there is an abrupt shift of narrative tone and focus precisely at this point in the paragraph. The shift is effected by a short statement from the narrator: "Nur ein einziger Gast war nicht zu erkennen" (56). In contrast to the series of clauses cited above which precedes it, and whose structural copiousness matches its subject matter (the wine, food, and socializing), this terse statement opens the way for the first detailed physical description of the poor pastor. The remainder of the passage balances shorter and longer sentences in a mixture of physical details and psychological insights into his character:

> Lächelnd und freundlich saß er da, er hörte aufmerksam alles an, er wandte immer das Angesicht der Gegend, wo eifrig gesprochen wurde, zu, als ob eine Pflicht ihn dazu antriebe, seine Mienen gaben allen Redenden recht, und wenn an einem andern Orte das Gespräch wieder lebhafter wurde, wandte er sich dorthin, und hörte zu. Selber aber sprach er kein Wort. Er saß ziemlich weit unten, und seine schwarze Gestalt ragte über das weiße Linnengedecke der Tafel empor, und obwohl er nicht groß war, so richtete er sich nie vollends auf, als hielte er das für unschicklich. Er hatte den Anzug eines armen Landgeistlichen. Sein Rock war sehr abgetragen, die Faden waren daran sichtbar, er glänzte an manchen Stellen, und an andern hatte er die schwarze Farbe verloren, und war rötlich oder fahl.(56)

The point-counterpoint of the imagery is unmistakable. The poor pastor is congenial, but his behavior seems forced; he listens attentively, but makes no utterances himself; he is seated far down the table, yet his black-garbed figure looms conspicuously above the white tablecloth; he is not tall, but he feels the need to sit modestly stooped in his chair; his black attire appears imposing at first, but it is actually threadbare and faded. This is the description of a character whose relationship with society is decidedly ambiguous. The priest is also shown here to be self-conscious and his self-consciousness will become, thematically speaking, more revealing than the paradoxical descriptive details cited above. At any rate, the interplay of ego, initiative, and socialization is clearly manifest in this brief depiction of a solitary figure who stands out primarily because his appearance and comportment indicate that he has not been fully assimilated into the group. It is also in the last half of the second paragraph that two important motifs make their first appearance. The pastor's cassock is faded to an almost reddish-gray hue, a shade which is often used later in the narrative to describe the dominant color of his barren but beloved limestone hills. This pale color of the cassock and of limestone comes to be symbolical of the pastor's ambiguous identity in the story and hence of the variation presented in "Kalkstein" of the interplay of ego, initiative, and socialization. And yet, if the color is faded, what might be the meaning of the "black" figure looming above the "white" tablecloth, and later towards the paragraph's end, of the conspicuously small, "white" lappets which hang over the priest's collar and which attest to his dignity (57)? The apparent explanation is, that the descriptions in this passage are a protracted paradox which serves as an imaginal complement to the philosophical and theoretical questions raised in the novella's first paragraph. There is, for example, in these banquet images the picture of a single personality at variance with the majority of his fellows, yet holding the attention of at least one thoughtful observer. There is also a discrepancy between the abilities [Fähigkeiten] which could be conventionally ascribed to a person in such a social position and his actual behavior and appearance. And, the reiteration in terms of color imagery likewise offers no easy answer to the philosophical paradox of human gifts and abilities.

In two concise sentences, Stifter introduces the important "linen" motif near the end of the second paragraph: ". . . bei den Ärmeln gingen, wie er so saß, manchmal ein ganz klein wenig eine Art Handkrausen hervor, die er immer bemüht war wieder heimlich zurück zu schieben. Vielleicht waren sie in einem Zustande, daß er sich ihrer ein wenig hätte schämen müssen" (57). Just as the earlier images of the white tablecloth and lappets can be viewed from a thematic viewpoint as symbolic of social acceptability and a successful and ritualized accommodation to social interaction, so too can the pastor's attempt at hiding his cuffs be seen as an indication of an ego-generated mode of behavior. Along with the narrative details which express the thematic interplay, Stifter has taken care to introduce a description of the pastor's sleeves which employs diminutives ("ein ganz klein wenig"; "ein wenig") to create ambivalence. A resolution of this ambivalence is then suspended by a tonal use of the subjunctive to distance the narrator from the explanation he himself offers for the priest's secretive behavior. At this point, the paragraph closes with a return to an observed series of actions carried out by the pastor. These actions continue and reinforce the hitherto developed characterization of him as an ego isolated from its society but involved in ritualized and openly constrained activities and initiatives which nonetheless express deference to that same society. Contextually the final lines of the novella's second paragraph form a narrative unit with the three shorter paragraphs which follow it. Their content effects a reversal of the descent-integration-socialization sequence depicted during the surveyor's arrival in the first half of the passage. After the thematically pregnant interruption provided by the detailed description of the pastor's appearance and idiosyncratic preoccupation with his shirt cuffs, the descriptive focus again settles upon his behavior at the banquet. The contrast of the double characterization (i.e., surveyor vs. pastor) continues (57). Where the surveyor had reached his highest point of social integration amidst sumptuous dinner courses and flowing wine, the pastor begins his gradual disengagement from the festivities by partaking only minimally of the fare and beverage. There is even a clear indication that the cleric consciously distances himself from the society, when he declines to prepare the customary take-home sampler of desserts for his dependents as a token of the ceremony (57). There then follow more descriptive details of his appearance, including mention of his stockings, faded from black to gray, and his heavy shoes, all of which continue the image of a somewhat awkward self-containment and isolation. He stands apart from the chatting groups of banqueters with his back against a window frame in a clear image of attitudinal separation which prefigures his actual physical departure in the following paragraph. It is not surprising that this problematical character is described in the subjunctive mood as "einer der . . . sich bereits den fünfzig Jahren nähere, oder Sorge und Kummer gehabt haben müsse"; and it is predictably "nach kurzer Zeit" that the pastor collects his cane and formally bids his host goodbye (57). The subjunctive is again used in his catalogue of excuses for leaving early. But there is also a hint of tacit acceptance of this character's complicated social orientation in the easy farewell he receives from his brother priest. In addition, the closing images of the paragraph mirror contrastively the surveyor's arrival by tracing the pastor's ascent through productive fields to the untilled hills beyond. The company presumably watches this departure from the same vantage point (the window) which provided the surveyor with his initial view of the gathering. The short paragraph which then follows brings the structural unit full circle by functioning as the narrative complement of the surveyor's self-introduction at the beginning of the second paragraph. The brevity, third person perspective, and subjunctive mood in the later introduction all contrast markedly, however, with its structural counterpart and enhance the paradoxical characterization of the protagonist developed in the first four pages of the work:

Der Hausherr fragte ihn, ob er denn schon gehen wolle, worauf er antwortete, es sei für ihn schon Zeit, er habe vier Stunden nach seinem Pfarrhofe zu gehen, und seine Füße seien nicht mehr so gut, wie in jüngeren Jahren. Der Pfarrer hielt ihn nicht auf. Er empfahl sich allseitig, ging zur Tür hinaus, und gleich darauf sahen wir ihn durch die Kornfelder dahin wandeln, den Hügel, der das Dorf gegen Sonnenuntergang begrenzte, hinan steigen, und dort gleichsam in die glänzende Nachmittagsluft verschwinden. Ich fragte, wer der Mann wäre, und erfuhr, daß er in einer armen Gegend Pfarrer sei, daß er schon sehr lange dort sei, daß er nicht weg verlange, und daß er selten das Haus verlasse außer bei einer sehr dringenden Veranlassung. (57–58)

As in "Granit," Stifter's use of the subjunctive mood here for indirect reportage is not grammatically extraordinary. Stylistically however, the decision to convey at this point in the narrative so many details of characterization in that mode seems to complement an aura of ambiguity. And as the story continues, it will be seen that the ambiguous characterization of the work's central figure is one of the chief narrational means for developing the variation manifest in "Kalkstein" of the tripartite thematic interplay of ego, initiative, and socialization.

The first four pages of "Kalkstein," then, form together what could be termed a "psychological preface," introducing the reader to the concept of an only partially socialized ego whose idiosyncratic initiatives will provide the narrative base for the remainder of the work. (The "atmospheric preface" of "Granit" created a social and evaluative framework within which an as yet incompletely socialized ego was prepared for the more complete process of integration which forms the narrative foundation of that novella.) Also it has been seen how the compositional elements of structure, style, and content work together to create this prefatory passage, presenting the thematically significant patterns which will be increasingly in evidence as the work continues its generally linear development of chronology, character, and theme.

At this point Stifter again shifts the time frame, but this time forward in the time of the inner narrative:

> Es waren seit jenem Gastmahle viele Jahre vergangen, und ich hatte den Mann vollständig vergessen, als mich mein Beruf einmal in eine fürchterliche Gegend rief. Nicht daß Wildnisse Schlünde Abgründe Felsen und stürzende Wässer dort gewesen wären—das alles zieht mich eigentlich an—, sondern es waren nur sehr viele kleine Hügel da, jeder Hügel bestand aus nacktem grauem Kalksteine, der aber nicht, wie es oft bei diesem Gesteine der Fall ist, zerrissen war, oder steil abfiel, sondern in rundlichen breiten Gestalten auseinander ging, und an seinem Fuße eine, lange gestreckte Sandbank um sich herum hatte. Durch diese Hügel ging in großen Windungen ein kleiner Fluß Namens Zirder. Das Wasser des Flusses, das in der grauen und gelben Farbe des Steines und Sandes durch den Widerschein des Himmels oft dunkelblau erschien, dann die schmalen grünen Streifen, die oft am Saume des Wassers hingingen, und die andern einzelnen

Rasenflecke, die in dem Gesteine hie und da lagen, bildeten die ganze Abwechslung und Erquickung in dieser Gegend. (58)

This shift in time frame and locale is given even more emphasis in the actual text of the novella through the end punctuation of the sentence and paragraph immediately preceding it—a period, followed by a dash.[2] One senses also the inherent paradox in the narrator's designation of the landscape as "fürchterlich," ["fearful"] when he follows it immediately with such concise descriptive details, even if they are not patently beautiful in a conventional sense. (Stifter the landscape artist scarcely conceals his enthusiasm here.) The surveyor's declaration that he would, in fact, welcome more dramatic and hence more dangerous geological features, such as cliffs and crevasses only continues the irony. This passage is, of course, an introduction to the thematically symbolic physical setting for most of the remaining story. Its also continues the concise outline of the major elements of personality and attitude of its two main figures, with an ensuing delineation and analysis of their respective characters to develop the surveyor as a suitable narrative foil for the pastor. The problematic nature of the novella's thematic variation is foreshadowed here in the surveyor's paradoxical perception of the "Steinkar" ["stoney basin"], a landscape which is thematically linked to the character of the "completely forgotten" pastor who has been there many years and rarely leaves the place. The ambivalence in the attitude of the surveyor, which is germinal but unmistakable, seems enhanced also by the use in this passage of the indicative mood. It will be noted in this regard that Stifter also makes abundant use of the subjunctive mood in this section of the work, but likewise in an apparently conventional way. The actual effect of the conventional usage of these grammar modes in these passages of "Kalkstein" which depict the first face-to-face meeting of the two main characters seems to be an almost unconscious "second thought" on the part of an attentive reader. One might even feel a corresponding ambivalence to match that of the character through whose eyes one views the proceedings. Such an attitudinal correspondence can prepare one by proxy, so to speak, for the thematic statement or can at least focus attention on thematically significant revelations. By manipulating the use of normal expressive modes in narrative contexts similar to those where he has used greater stylistic finesse, Stifter seems to evoke an irony which again demonstrates his ability to maintain his thematic base just below the surface of almost every passage of the novella. At this point in "Kalkstein," one begins to ascertain a linear version of the reiterative stylistic and structural techniques used in "Granit." This linear approach links passages of increasingly revelatory pertinence for the thematic interplay, which is always present but never explicitly suggested as in that first novella of *Bunte Steine*. Likewise the color motifs contribute to the forward narrative movement in "Kalkstein," with the neutral grey, in particular, assuming a broader and progressively more important symbolism as the dominant hue of the story's physical setting. As can be seen in the passage just cited, there is, again, a linear development from the use of color in the earlier-cited scene at the church celebration. There it served the narrower function of suggesting discrepancies between the appearance and station of the protagonist. Another recurrent, thematically supportive image should also be mentioned at this point: the river Zirder, whose orthographic and phonetic connotations nicely match its initial mention as the sole ornament in an otherwise dreary landscape (cf. *Zierde*). Considering the use earlier of the place name Schauendorf in the passage depicting the more visibly developed parish of the energetic orchardman/priest (cf. *Schau, Dorf*), Stifter presumably intends here to imbue the image of the river with a symbolic significance. The Zirder later becomes a key element in the identification of the poor pastor's chief initiative, which in turn permits the successful social integration of his ostensibly problematic ego and ultimately provides "Kalkstein" its philosophic variation of the common thematic interplay in *Bunte Steine*. It is thus interesting to note as the narrative proceeds, how the structural, stylistic, and imaginal elements just described gradually gain in clarity and thematic import. Within the context of the two-pronged character development they narratively sublimate the compressed personalities of both the protagonist and his opposite number, the surveyor. This process itself represents the thematic explication of a view of life and reality wherein human subtleties and ambiguities are played out against and ironically highlighted by a seemingly passive physical background.

The second meeting between the surveyor/narrator and the poor pastor, which initiates the next narrative phase of the novella, is preceded by two short paragraphs which delineate in an increasingly pointed manner the contrastive characters of the two major figures (58–59). The surveyor states that he has taken lodgings at an inn in a geographically marginal and, consequently, somewhat better part of the "fearful" region. This inn is located on the "Hochstraße" ["high road"] and is situated on higher ground than the Steinkar, with its monotonous, weathered limestone formations and shallow river basin. The evaluative implications of the high-low imagery evoked here in the surveyor's descriptions are reinforced by his statement that to avoid wasting time in transit, he takes a cold lunch to the distant work site and eats his major meal of the day in the evening when he returns to the Hochstraße. He states in the same context that, while some of his work crew reside above with him, there are some who have erected makeshift wooden shanties at the site below. These details underscore not only the general lack of enthusiasm expressed by the surveyor for the region, but they also leave open the possibility of a later rapprochement between high and low. As a dutiful leader, the surveyor may be called upon to join his workers in closer physical proximity to the jobsite. This does, in fact, occur; but for the time being Stifter suspends any too direct consideration of the thematic significance of such a situation. He again accentuates the negativity of the narrator's perceptions by having him state that the region's general isolation is due not to any inordinate distance from population centers, but rather because there is little motivation for anyone to go there.

The description of the poor priest in the paragraph which follows the passages just outlined is less ambiguous than the one in the banquet scene, although at first it continues along the lines established in that earlier description. The surveyor catches sight of his long-forgotten acquaintance, the threadbare pastor, sitting reflectively one evening on a sandpile in the "Kar," or river basin:

> Er hatte seine großen Schuhe fast in den Sand vergraben, und auf den Schößen seines Rockes lag Sand. Ich erkannte ihn in dem Augenblicke. Er war ungefähr so gekleidet wie damals, als ich ihn zum ersten Male gesehen hatte. Seine Haare waren jetzt viel grauer, als hätten sie sich beeilt diese Farbe anzunehmen, sein längliches Angesicht hatte deutliche Falten bekommen, und nur die Augen waren blau und klar wie früher. An seiner Seite lehnte das Rohr mit dem schwarzen Beinknopfe. (59)

This description is developed around two complementary images which, nonetheless, call up distinctive aspects of the pastor's character. The first image is that of an almost corporeally sympathetic integration of the pastor with the same physical setting just delineated so ambivalently by the surveyor. His feet are buried in the sand and his coattails are partially covered also. He forms an extension of the sandpile he is seated upon; yet the second image developed in this paragraph hearkens back to the earlier description of him as an obtrusive presence in the surveyor's recollection of the church celebration. The pastor's attire and expression are hardly changed, even to the detail of the walking cane, which will be remembered from that earlier scene as a symbol of an *Einzelgänger*. His hair, however, is described as being much grayer. Again the use of this color motif to express the ambivalence of the surveyor towards the pastor can be sensed; although several years have passed since their last encounter, the surveyor perceives this particular change as being sudden, even willful (59). At several later points in the story, Stifter also refers in unclear terms to the passage of time as it relates to his protagonist.

Along with the continuation of earlier images, wherein his previous description is made to coalesce with the new view of the pastor as an integral part of his gray limestone surroundings, this passage communicates an embryonic awareness in the surveyor that his overall perception of the poor pastor will be modified. When the ongoing dialogue between the pastor and surveyor begins in earnest, their initial exchange is conveyed in direct discourse, the first use of that stylistic mode in "Kalkstein." This approach moves the theoretical and objective observations of the surveyor into the realm of personal experience, and the direct speech is equally revealing of his own character as well as of the psychology of the poor pastor. Stifter appears to to contrast and balance the two figures in this passage by such means as word choice, the textual near-duplication of passages, and the alternation of indicative and subjunctive tonalities within the same passage. An instance of selective word choice is the use of the term "hesitate" ["innehalten"] to indicate the surveyor's growing self-consciousness upon finally meeting the object of his earlier reflections. The pastor is then described as "hurried" ["eilfertig"] in his response to the unexpected greeting. The respective connotations of hesitancy and eagerness contained in these two terms seem to foreshadow a reversal of hitherto established attitudes, a reversal which in turn will open the way for a more intimate communication between the two characters. The surveyor, who was depicted in his own words as gregariously integrated into the festivities of the consecration celebration, is now ill at ease in a strange landscape as he hesitantly embarks upon an attempt at sociability. He openly recalls that the pastor was less concerned with observing him at the banquet than the reverse. This statement fits the facts, it is true, but the way it is uttered, using subjunctive forms and coming at a narrative juncture already replete with tonal ambivalence, seems to continue the gradual depiction of the surveyor as the "odd-man-out." The surveyor also declares, again with his newly acquired selfconsciousness, that it is the pastor's polite tone which he himself adopts in their introductory chat. But in reality, it is the surveyor who begins the sequence with the highly formalized "Euer Ehrwürden" ["your reverence"]. The pastor does use the word "Ehre" ["honor"] in replying to the suggestion that he has forgotten the surveyor: "Ich bin nicht der Ehre teilhaftig." But it is the surveyor who uses derivatives of the form "Ehre" four times in the next few paragraphs in addressing the pastor. The terms of reverence applied to a cleric are not unusual in themselves, but the surveyor's self-conscious explanation for using them seems more calculated to reveal his own uncertainty than to describe the actual facts of the situation. His uncertainty is also highlighted by the structural pairing of two paragraphs which express exactly the same material: the first, from the surveyor's viewpoint and primarily in the subjunctive; the second, in the first person from the viewpoint of the pastor and consistently in the indicative (60).

Such a sequential duplication seems at first almost narratively clumsy in its contrast of respective recollections by the two main characters of the same event, the pastor's low-key but nonetheless somewhat obtrusive departure from the church celebration. Stifter, however, has once again added enough structural and stylistic variation to an apparently redundant passage to continue his linear narrative flow. It seems obvious when the pastor systematically affirms the surveyor's recollections in the subjunctive of his earlier actions that the pastor is making no excuses. He states unequivocally that he viewed his attendance at the festivities as a professional obligation to a fellow cleric, and he ends with a pointed admission that he has not returned to Schauendorf since. The suspensive ambiguity is still present as well in the irony that the surveyor should not also remember the possibility of the pastor's long-term connection with the Steinkar. Such a connection was explicit in the details of his life which the surveyor elicited from others at the end of their first meeting in Schauendorf—not to mention the fact that we would expect a surveyor to be able to at least roughly calculate the relationships among the direction of a departure and the time span and the distance on foot required for its destination, to arrive at the reasonable assumption that the pastor had possibly been a resident of the Kar at the time of their first encounter. To assume a compositional lapse here on the part of the author, however, would be to underestimate Stifter's ability to creatively manipulate his material. The surveyor is, at worst, displaying his own particular brand of unequally developed "Geistesgaben," as per the philosophical pronouncements which opened the novella. At best, his basic nature is being refined or sublimated in keeping with his development as a characterizational foil for the protagonist of the piece. One begins to note a sort of glibness in the personality of the surveyor which contrasts markedly with the natural sincerity and evaluative depth of the pastor's reply to his derogatory assessment of the surrounding area. The pastor says, "Sie ist, wie sie Gott erschaffen hat, . . . es wachsen hier nicht so viele Bäume wie in Schauendorf, aber manches Mal ist sie auch schön, und zuweilen ist sie schöner als alle andern in der Welt" (60). It is noteworthy here that the pastor makes a pointed contrast between his beloved Steinkar and the village of Schauendorf. This is in fact the fourth utterance of the name "Schauendorf" in as many paragraphs, and it seems possible that in the pastor's view, the trees of that place are symbolic of ostentatious individual initiative, in that the foliation alluded to was principally the work of one man, the orchardman/priest of Schauendorf. A subtle criticism of socialization in the form of collective egoism could likewise be implied in the word play present in the place name (cf. "Show Village"). At any rate, the poor pastor significantly contrasts the humanly modified landscape of Schauendorf with the natural, divinely ordered character of the basin region, or Kar, to the advantage of the latter. In terms of the overall narrative format of "Kalkstein," the point-counterpoint expressed in this first conversation between the work's two main characters shows the two-pronged process of characterization to be fully underway. This process, as was mentioned earlier, will systematically involve the simultaneous revelation and analysis of both personalities and a clarification of the apparently simple character behind the pastor's personal initiatives. This dual dynamic in the novella's structure will ultimately enable an exposition of the subtlety and complexity of the thematic interplay of ego, initiative, and socialization which binds the work together.

Having once established his narrative technique, Stifter then manipulates it to slow the story's forward momentum and to enable some embellishment and refinement of what could otherwise be an incompletely developed premise. As if the thematically significant features of the protagonist's psychology were becoming too readily obvious at this point, the dialogue ends with a paragraph of predominantly indirect discourse which reiterates in ironically innocuous style most of the factual points already stated by the surveyor: the pastor is settled ["ansässig"] in the Steinkar, he has been there a very long time, the surveyor is living on the fringe of the region, etc. (60). This paragraph, representing as it does a structural, stylistic and contextual "pulling back," nonetheless recapitulates neatly the elements of characterization pointing toward the sublimation of the story's main personage or ego. But, as if to reassert the stylistic approach which for most of the tale maintains the ambiguity of the characterization, the paragraph ends with one final direct quote from the pastor in which he indicates his attachment to the region by admitting to habitual wanderings among the limestone outcroppings. One is reminded here of Stifter's ability (so evident in "Granit") to proceed structurally, stylistically, and imaginally through his narrative gathering substance for his underlying thematic design, and then to suspend that accumulated momentum in preparation for the next forward movement of the plot.[3] Also apparent is his willingness to segment the balance of momentum and retardation within even the smallest structural units, as he has done with the two lines of direct discourse at the end of this first "conversational" passage between the two main characters in the novella.

The following page begins with a brief allusion to continued chatting about indifferent ["gleichgültigen"] things such as the weather and the seasons (61). And there is a perhaps meaningful but indirect mention of the light-absorptive qualities of the surrounding limestone formations. But the passage soon refocuses upon a renewed reflection in the first person by the surveyor on the problematic significance of the pastor's threadbare appearance. The surveyor expresses again his ambivalence towards this apparent eccentricity by describing the pastor's attire as being even more worn than before. His hat is particularly shocking, being without any nap. The image of the younger man involuntarily but repeatedly glancing at the older man's worn head covering continues to reestablish the ambiguity of characterization and the narrative suspense which was just beginning at the end of the preceding page. There is also a brief reassertion of the two-pronged characterization, with the insertion of a narratively logical and at the same time thematically consistent passage between two paragraphs of the surveyor's ambivalence-laden reflections: "Als wir an die Stelle gelangt waren, wo sein Weg sich von dem meiningen trennte, und zu seinem Pfarrhofe in das Kar hinab führte, nahmen wir Abschied, und sprachen die Hoffnung aus, daß wir uns nun öfter treffen würden" (61). The image of the parting ways and of the pastor's descent keeps the characterization contrastive, but there is an unmistakable note of potential compatibility expressed in the hope for future encounters.

The intimation of narrative progress is characteristically qualified by the stylistic choice of a subjunctive form (rather than an infinitive construction, for instance) to end the lines quoted above. The characterizational ambiguity is then given summary expression in the following stylistically, imaginally, and structurally balanced paragraph: the surveyor ascends to the Hochstrasse, but he thinks of the pastor down below. The poverty of the cleric's appearance is unusual ["ungemein"], even beggarly. This thought is pointedly described as becoming a constant ["beständige"] preoccupation of the narrator. The pastor is actually scrupulously clean ["ängstlich reinlich"], but this only highlights his threadbare attire all the more. The surveyor finds this perceptual dilemma painfully embarassing ["peinlich"]. The terms "impermanent" ["unhaltbar"] and "unsubstantial" ["wesenlos"] designate the chief characteristics of the pastor's clothing, and the surveyor turns, as if to find some evaluative counter-image, to the panorama of the landscape. But he perceives the hills as "nur mit Stein bedeckt" and the valleys as adorned only by the long sandbanks (61). It is clear that the narrator is struggling with the ambiguities replete in the unconventional appearance of the poor pastor, and with the ambivalence of his own feelings toward the physical surroundings. There is some structural relief expressed in the surveyor's decision to retreat to his inn, "um den Ziegenbraten zu verzehren, den sie mir dort öfter vorsetzten" (61). Yet, Stifter's ability to manipulate even the smallest of compositional elements to create or maintain a contextual tension seems once again evident in the pairing of the words "meinen" and "Gasthof" with their contrastive connotations of possession and transcience, and in the somewhat stylized use of the comparative "öfter".

But is there any discernible forward progress in this narrative back-and-forth which promotes further development of the thematic interplay of ego, initiative, and socialization? The first and last elements of the interplay are certainly present throughout this passage, as they are in those preceding it. One need only consider the self-revealing reflections of the surveyor about the local geography, his almost obsessive concern with the pastor's appearance, and the pastor's brief expression of his somewhat isolationist views to sense an undercurrent of egocentrism on several psychological levels. The surveyor's tacit perception of himself as an active agent of organized society, his uncertainty about the suitability of his rediscovered acquaintance as a social model, and his at least tentative attachment to the local society as represented by his inn, all express the general concept of socialization. The thematic component of initiative is, it must be admitted, conspicuously slight at this point in the novella. But this only confirms the view that it is a problematic, more complex variation of the thematic interplay which is being developed in "Kalkstein." The positive potentialities of the pastor exhibited directly or indirectly in this passage point toward an increasing readiness on the part of the surveyor (and vicariously on the part of the reader as well?) to look beyond surface conventionalities in evaluating that character's initiatives toward ego-societal integration, should they become manifest. The passage ends with the final tipping of the analytical scale implicit in the solicitousness of the surveyor's decision to forego inquiries at the inn about the priest, "um keine rohe Antwort zu bekommen" (61). The pastor's initiatives will come to the fore as the story progresses. But the author maintains the gradual, narratively logical development which is in keeping with the complexity of the thematic variation in "Kalkstein." Unlike "Granit," in which several separate proofs of a basic ego-initiative-socialization dynamic were developed and accumulated, Stifter must here prepare the way for a more refined perception of such an interplay, which will be fully exhibited only in two closely connected situations. In this same regard, the character of the pastor cannot assume any overtly didactic features, as in the case of the grandfather in "Granit," because the analytical focus will be upon his own actions and reactions, and not those of others. Hence, the characterization of both main characters continues on but does narrow to that of the pastor ultimately, providing an inferred moral supportive of the novella's thematic variation. The next structurally and contextually distinguishable section of the text, which extends for some two pages (62–63), depicts in general terms the growing friendship between the surveyor and the pastor, with a growing inclination on the part of the former to view the eccentricities of the latter in a less ambivalent, more accepting manner.

The surveyor sets an accomodative tone for this passage by stating: "Von nun an kam ich öfter mit dem Pfarrer zusammen" (61). He still feels the need to offer an ostensibly logical explanation for the situation, asserting that his surveying activities and the pastor's "occasional" outings make it a matter of unavoidable causality that they should meet. But on closer examination his explanation stands in contrast to other attitudinal indicators in the same paragraph. The "rather often" ["öfter"] of the opening sentence hardly corresponds with the "occasionally" ["zuweilen"] used to describe the pastor's visits to the work area. The choice of the terms "rambled around" ["schlenderte"] and "get to know" ["kennenlernen"], in regard to the surveyor's methods and motivations for studying his surroundings seem to express a more reflective than systematic orientation to the purported task at hand. The pastor in his turn seems to view their meetings not without pleasure ["nicht ungerne"], and the surveyor comes upon his new acquaintance in the Kar, or basin region also with pleasure (62). The connotations inherent in these expressions of frequency and enthusiasm are quickly assimilated to thematically supportive natural images when the narrator gives a general but nonetheless itemized account of their meetings:

> Wir gingen später öfter mit einander in den Steinen herum, oder saßen auf einem, und betrachteten die andern. Er zeigte mir manches Tierchen, manche Pflanze, die der Gegend eigentümlich waren, er zeigte mir die Besonderheiten der Gegend, und machte mich auf die Verschiedenheiten mancher Steinhügel aufmerksam, die der sorgfältigste Beobachter für ganz gleich gebildet angesehen haben würde   Ich erzählte ihm von meinen Reisen, zeigte ihm unsere Werkzeuge, und erklärte ihm bei Gelegenheit unserer Arbeiten manchmal deren Gebrauch. (62)

One is reminded here of the tutelage rendered by the kindly patriarch in "Granit," yet the scope seems much more focused and detailed. The diminutive "Tierchen," and the various other terms ("Pflanze," "eigentümlich," "Besonderheiten," "Verschiedenheiten," "sorgfältigsten") all point toward a closer scrutiny which contrasts with the panoramic vistas in "Granit." And, as already mentioned above, Stifter is careful to maintain the surveyor's function as a credible foil—hence his reciprocal tutelage of the pastor in the ways of surveying. The tension between the surveyor's rationalizations and openly declared enjoyment of his new friendship, together with the imagery of perceptual detail contained in this paragraph, seem to continue the process of his psychological preparation for a later evaluation of the poor pastor's initiatives. There is only a perfunctory allusion to what might be called socially oriented initiative in the matter-of-fact enumeration of the surveyor's conversational topics. The clauses delineating "our work" ["unsere Arbeit"] are clearly outweighed textually and in terms of imagery by the pastor's contributions to their hillside forum. The thematic exposition is still analytically weighted toward the ego component of the tripartite interplay at this point, with only slight manifestations of the socialization and initiative components.

The next paragraph seems at first perusal to be constructed to rectify the dearth of development in the thematic element of initiative (62). It follows immediately the outline of the surveyor's tutorial demonstrations and depicts the parsonage and grounds which should be the site of some of the pastor's actual work. Thus, there should also be a noticeable textual contrast with the natural musings and observations he formulated in the rocky landscape as cited above. Such turns out not to be the case, and the actual effect of this paragraph is to continue the development of images, motifs and perceptions to aid in the creation of a psychological atmosphere. Already established spatial and temporal connotative values are visibly mixed in the first sentence: The surveyor reports that he has several times (a positive connotation by dint of habituation) gone "down" (a negative spatial connotation) with the pastor to his parsonage (a positive religious connotation, which also reflects on the personal connection expressed by the possessive). The actual sequence of these connotative elements is "einige Male" to "seinen Pfarrhof" to "hinunter" —two positives to effect a perceptual modification of a subsequent negative. This spatial pattern is repeated in the very next line, as the pair of characters is described as proceeding from the point where "das stärkste Gestein sich ein wenig auflöset," across a "sänftere Abdachung" "hinab" to the basin (62). In spite of, or more properly along with the pairings of strength and stone (which itself has already become an ambivalent symbol) with dissolution, and of mildness and sheltering with the hitherto foreboding phenomenon of the low-lying basin area, there is an unmistakable descriptive movement towards imaginal softening. The connotatively pregnant spatial and phenomenal amalgamation continues as the narrative perspective moves from the "Rande der Gesteine," to a meadow with several trees, and then to a giant linden tree, and finally to the parsonage behind it. Color motifs, two already specific to the story and one new one with similarly universal value, complete the positive depiction. The parsonage is white and makes a lovely contrast with the friendly green of the vegetation, as well as with the gray of the bordering rocks. The setting seems to characterize its occupant, who by virtue of his priesthood should provide a connecting point for the parish's physical survival as well as for its spiritual affairs. Yet, it is once again the problematic aspect of the pastor which is expressed ultimately in this passage. The closing lines of the paragraph revert to an ambiguous, if not tacitly negative imagery, which seems more explicitly expressive of the pastor's initiatives and professional activities than of his conventionally socialized image, as symbolized by the exterior of the parsonage. The image of the trees may still be evocative of Schauendorf and the orchardist, toward both of which the "poor pastor" has already shown only formalized civility. It is the church and school which would logically provide the theater for most of the pastor's initiatives, and yet they are respectively described here as being hidden among the outcroppings and located in "einem dürftigen Garten" (62). It semms also significant that although the three public structures comprise the nucleus of the basin community, the scattered habitations of the local people share the somber descriptive imagery of the latter two buildings, being "an manchem Stein gleichsam angeklebt" and having only a potato bed and goat fodder patch here and there (62). It is only "weit draußen gegen das Land hin" that the truly productive communal acreage is located. Thus, this paragraph can be seen to maintain obliquely the ambiguity in the character of the pastor; yet the narrative momentum seems to be towards an ever more explicit clarification of focus and towards the inclusion of the component of initiative in the thematic interplay of ego, initiative, and socialization.

Although the pastor has until now done nothing specific in the way of a personal initiative which might be evaluated from a social viewpoint, the novella's next passage prefigures the first of two such initiatives to come. The river Zirder, which was previously lauded as the landscape's only adornment, is here referred to as the "einsamer Fluß" ["solitary river"] over which a high footbridge descends to the low shore opposite the parsonage. The bridge is a symbol of socialized effort in the communal interest, and its significance for both of the individualized initiatives of the pastor will become apparent later in the story. The passage ends with two paragraphs of approximately equal length and detail (63). The first of the pair balances, almost expectedly, the foregoing preponderance of obliquely positive images of characterization with a series of similarly indirect ones which reiterate the egocentric aspects of the main character. The surveyor/narrator notes that he is never taken to the upper story of the parsonage during his visits and that the lower story is only sparsely and poorly furnished. There is a large, leather-bound Bible on a wooden bench along one wall, and a rickety table and chairs. The concept of a sincere rejection of worldly accouterments by an earnest Christian minister is, of course, consistent with these details. But considering the physically attractive nature of the exterior of the dwelling and the presence of two yellow cabinets and a small but "sehr schön aus Birnholz geschnitztes mittelalterliches Crucifix" amidst the general bareness, one cannot help but sense only incomplete austerity with hints of a socially conventional, outward deference to the status of the office. There also seems to be some former connection with a more well-to-do lifestyle. Stifter's stylistic subtlety is again evident here, in the ironic attempt by the surveyor to downplay the detail of the obtrusively fine crucifix. Using the subjunctive, he states that in assessing the overall paucity of the inner rooms, one would have to except this particularly fine artifact (63).

The intimations of egocentricity become explicit in the final paragraph of this section, with the reappearance of the "linen" motif. The narrator remembers the pastor's cuff-hiding behavior from years before, and adds to his recollection now the "strange discovery" that the pastor's sleeves are paradoxically the finest and cleanest he has ever seen. The ambivalent tone created by several subjunctives in these lines also supports the idea that the thematic aspect of the ego and its implicit complexities is being revived. But the concentration of connotatively positive words such as "untadelhaft," "weiß," "Reinheit," "Besorgung," and "Sorgfalt" in relation to the pastor's idiosyncratic behavior, coming at the end of the paragraph as it does, gives final expression to the generally forward-looking tone of this entire two-page section of text. The surveyor's final assertion that he doesn't intrude upon the pastor's reticence on this delicate matter, as quite a matter of course, is another intentionally ironic support (considering his admission that he very frequently peers at the garments in question) for the dual characterization of these two figures which keeps the narrative moving. In summation, these passages appear to exhibit the recurrent pattern established in the novella of elucidating or narratively sublimating problematic and complex aspects of the story's main protagonist through the perceptions and interactions of a characterizational foil. As some progress towards an actual explication of this interesting ego is assured, just enough dubiety is reaffirmed to create suspense about the next cycle of structure, image, and text which will move us further in the same direction. The narrative takes two steps forward and one back as it moves toward a very thorough, unquestionable exposition of a unique ego and the dilemma of assessing this self's initiatives towards socialization. The author effects a narrative shift at this point with the structural device of inserting a simple, contextually summative statement between two longer paragraphs. Indented in the text, in the manner of an independent paragraph, is the surveyor/narrator's simple statement: "Unter diesem Verkehre ging ein Teil des Sommers dahin" (63). From here follows an extended series of passages covering some fourteen full pages of text which in content are a duplication of the immediately preceding sections. There is the same pairing of the two main characters in the natural setting of the "Steingegend," ["the stoney sector"] from whence the narrative locale again is moved downward to the parsonage on the meadow below. There is also a similar emphasis on the dual characterization of the surveyor and the pastor, but some procedural differences in the two sections seem apparent. The process of revealing or sublimating the two major characters (with that of the pastor, as always, slightly predominant) is actuated in this latter section, not by general observations, actions, and reactions spread over an undefined time frame, as was the case earlier. There is instead a much more specific concentration on situations related in a detailed and causal manner which transpire within the space of one afternoon and evening and the following morning. The thematic progress or "step forward" which appears in turn to develop here involves a gradual increase in the number of specific, individualized physical actions or initiatives. This general increase will in turn focus, in the section of the text immediately subsequent to the one being considered here, on a timely narration of the first thematically critical initiative by the protagonist.

The surveyor has released his crew around midday due to an unnaturally hot and hazy weather front which has settled over the area. There is only a half-sunlight, which nonetheless produces the discomfort of "drei Tropensonnen" (64). These eerily foreboding conditions persist towards evening, and the reader senses a gathering storm (and perhaps a concomitant energizing of the narrative action). As regards characterization, it is interesting to note that the surveyor seeks refuge from the misery not in his inn on the Hochstraße as usual, but rather under a rock overhang in the boulder strewn "Steingegend" itself. The image of the rocks as a haven, rather than as the earlier object of distaste is also supported by the brief, but for the first time graphic depiction of the surveyor eating there rather than at the inn. It was stated earlier, to be sure, that lunching in the rocks was part of his daily routine, but here, significantly, it is one of only three literally enumerated actions or initiatives in the paragraph. The other two actions mentioned are reading and wandering, both of which reflect the psychological accommodation the surveyor has undergone in regard to the physical setting which had seemed so inimical to his character earlier. Fittingly, the character most connected with the region, the poor pastor, appears at the end of the paragraph, lending additional support to the accommodative tone of the passage. There are also contextual juxtapositions and stylistic support for this tone in the pastor's polite, subjunctively phrased inquiry about the surveyor's professional (i.e., conventionally socialized) endeavors for the day. The surveyor passes quickly over this query to end the paragraph with his almost eager admission that he has been relaxing under the overhang with a book. The two men walk on together, and the central topic of conversation for the next several passages is the approaching storm. The pastor's first statement on this point contains an ironic prediction: "Es wird nicht mehr möglich sein, daß Sie die Hochstraße erreichen" (64). In truth, the attitudinal ambivalence of the surveyor toward the pastor, symbolized in part by his earlier selection of a personal abode only marginally connected with the Kar, is all but resolved at this point in the story. And he will no longer be able to remain on the perceptual or evaluative "fringe" with regard to the pastor.

It is, of course, the weather conditions to which the narrative surface of the pastor's prediction refers. The discussion between the surveyor and pastor now runs the gamut from scientific and philosophical observations by the former on the provenance of precipitation to experience-based assessments by the latter of the proximity and severity of the storm. This conversational dichotomy continues the dual characterization of the two men, depicting the surveyor in general terms as the representative of a broad-based, socially conventional education while the cleric is seen as the possessor of a more narrowly focused natural wisdom. The question of which of these two configurations of spiritual and mental gifts ["Geistesgaben"] is most pertinent in considering major individual initiatives will provide the ultimate framework for completing the thematic variation present in "Kalkstein." But in the section of text being analyzed here, these contrasting viewpoints serve as a narrative backdrop for a series of lesser but cumulatively relevant actions and reactions on the part of the two main characters. The first of the initiatives involves a decision by the surveyor to heed the pastor's warnings and accept his offer of refuge from the storm. The pair have approached the edge of the rocks, and the vivid depiction of a building thunderstorm reveals Stifter's much-praised talent for natural description. The descent to the parsonage is described in almost identical connotative terms as those evoked in the preceding section: "Wir schlugen also den Weg in das Kar ein, und gingen über den sanften Steinabhang in die Wiese hinunter" (66). After another descriptive paragraph on the quickly building storm, the author effects a slight but significant shift of scene with a terse line: "Endlich gingen wir in das Haus" (67). Once the scene shifts inside the dwelling, the narrative context of the novella, which heretofore has involved for the most part only generally outlined activities such as walking and conversing, becomes notably more varied and detailed in the physical initiatives or actions depicted. The pastor leads his guest into the inner room of the parsonage and, after politely directing him to put down his carrying case and other personal effects, leaves the room and brings back a candle, brass holder, and a brass wicktrimmer in order to observe his usual method of waiting out a storm. The surveyor in his turn does doff his equipment, hangs his pouch on a chair, and leans his surveying rod against one of the pastor's yellow cabinets. One is again put in mind of a reversed image here, remembering the detail of the pastor's black-knobbed, reed walking stick in the consecration celebration passage. The surveyor is, at least in his own temporary perception of the situation, now the one who must deport himself successfully or not. This initial depiction of detailed activity is momentarily suspended when the two men sit quietly together for the duration of the downpour. The tempest, in apparent imaginal concert with the human scenario, also develops from vague, distant intimations of atmospheric activity to detailed occurrences—such as individualized raindrops striking against the panes, isolated gusts of wind, and shattering claps of thunder. As the storm climaxes and begins to abate, the surveyor describes the pastor as having sat "calmly and simply" ["ruhig und einfach"] through the entire proceedings. This is the external image of the pastor which has been developing from the beginning of the story, and it will remain an essentially valid one till the end. But the evaluative dilemma posed by his final initiative towards societal interaction will be anything but simple.

In advance of that initiative, the narrative continues with the depiction of numerous minor acts which are nonetheless revealing of character (69). The pastor lights another candle, leaves the room, and returns bearing a serving tray with items upon it meant for their supper. He sets down a milk pitcher from the tray and then pours out two glasses of milk. Then he sets down a green lacquered bowl full of strawberries and several pieces of black bread on a plate. Next he lays down a knife and a small spoon at each place, whereupon he takes the serving tray away again. It can be seen in this English paraphrase how much narrative space continues to be given to verbal and physical details in this section of the text. The page ends with another short paragraph describing the course and conclusion of the simple meal; the paragraph has only three sentences but no less than twelve independent clauses with single verbs. There then follow an additional page and a half of detailed actions depicting the surveyor's attempt at treating his host to some more varied refreshment, consisting of his lunch leftovers of sausage, cheese, roast, and even some ether-cooled wine. His preparations are just as meticulously described as were those of the pastor, but Stifter's instinct for suspensive balance in the interest of maintaining his thematic substratum seems present in the narrator's reference to the pastor at this particular juncture as "der arme Pfarrer" (70). This appellation reintroduces the contrastive characterization of the two main figures, as if that thematically suggestive contrast were in danger of being too readily and prematurely resolved in the narrative wake of all these detailed actions. But, as always with Stifter, what at first may appear as simple reiteration contains an element of development—a nuance, which, in this case furthers our understanding of the story's central personality. The "poor" pastor is attentive to his guest's ministrations, but consistent with his actions at the church celebration he declines all but a polite sampling of the proffered fare. The surveyor then stops eating also and reflects with an implied new insight into the character of his opposite number: "Ich . . . packte dann alles wieder zusammen, indem ich mich der Unhöflichkeit, die ich eigentlich in der Übereilung begangen hatte, schämte" (71). This rashness and subsequent embarrassment reminds one of the earlier faux-pax by the surveyor which elicited the pastor's aesthetic defense of the "Steinkar," or rocky river basin; but here the narrator is sensitive to his own mistake, and the pastor shows no sign of offense. As was the case in the earlier situation, the surveyor's perception is more important for an understanding of his own psychology than as a narrative element.

The balance of the dual characterization now swings back to the pastor, with another stylistic concentration of verbs depicting his preparation of a sleeping place for his guest. The "linen" motif also reappears when the surveyor carefully observes his host's preparations on his behalf:

> Dann öffnete er einen der gelben Schreine, (und) nahm ein Leintuch von außerordentlicher Schönheit Feinheit and Weiße heraus . . . Als ich bei dem schwachen Scheine der Kerze die ungemeine Trefflichkeit des Linnenstückes gesehen, und dann unwillkürlich meine Augen auf ihn gewendet hatte, errötete er in seinem Angesichte." (71)

The significance of the yellow cabinets is now revealed in connection with the pastor's eccentricity concerning his personal linens; and this detail consolidates the duplicative structure of the two passages. The spontaneity of the surveyor's questioning glance and the pastor's visible embarrassment are more convincing than the supposed discomfiture of the former mentioned in the context of the shared meal. At any rate, the narrative focus on the pastor's problematic ego continues, all accumulated positive virtues notwithstanding, as the surveyor becomes privy to the old cleric's odd sleeping habits. When the guest witnesses his host lying down for the night on a bare wooden bench with no covering and only his worn leather Bible for a headrest, the surveyor assumes he has inadvertently usurped the only bedding available. His protests about being professionally accustomed to roughing it and being determined not to impose are met with equanimity and friendly logic by the pastor. He assures his lodger that his own profession also has its accustomizing influence and it is in keeping with his station in life that he behave in such a way, not to mention that he does have additional bedding readily available (73). The egocentricity of this behavior is highlighted by the fact that the pastor sleeps covered only by his gray, full-length undergarments and gray socks. The symbolic ambiguity of this color fits well with the subsequent response of the surveyor who still hesitates mistrustfully after hearing the pastor's explanation.

But even as soon as the next clause, Stifter introduces the expected developmental, forward-moving impetus into his alternating narrative balance. The cleric replies in his turn, "Sie können in Ihrem Herzen ganz beruhigt sein, ganz beruhigt" (73). The pastor's natural assimilation of the disparate phenomena of station, logic, and heart reveals the essence of his personal psychology. It comprises a rare amalgam of professional integrity, practical determination, and emotional sincerity. The surveyor must then excuse his own protest on the basis of a conventional reaction, "Weil man gewöhnlich überall ein gebettetes Lager hat" (74). The pastor's final pronouncement on the matter contains a gently ironical, but still clear admonition to reflect upon this conventional outlook, when he says, "man . . . gewöhnt sich daran, und meint, es müsse so sein. Aber es kann auch anders sein. An alles gewöhnt sich der Mensch, und die Gewohnheit wird dann sehr leicht, sehr leicht" (74). The clarification of character Stifter effects here, particularly through the possible double entendre of the last line, encapsulates the thematic variation the pastor personifies in "Kalkstein": the conventional perception of the universal interplay of ego, initiative, and socialization must sometimes be modified to accommodate the unconventional case. The inherent question in such a premise (at least as it is presented in this novella) is: can the individual case be evaluated as worthy of such accommodation only on the basis of the successful integration of the three components of the interplay?

Up to this point, the author has depicted an ego in deliberately ambiguous terms, tightly juxtaposing imagery expressive of idiosyncrasy both in appearance and behavior, with revealing passages of dialogue and personal interaction expressive of a basically altruistic personality. The socialization component of the thematic interplay has been maintained for the most part by implications generated by the process of characterization. The same can generally be said about the initiative component as well, as both of these last analyzed paragraphs complement those which described the storm's advent. Thematically, however, the final image of this passage is perhaps the most significant. The Zirder has overflowed its banks and left the far side of the high footbridge submerged, along with a portion of the meadow beyond (76). It is interesting to note here that the usually so prominent grayness of the limestone is now simply one harmonious element along with the green of the meadow, the silvery surface of the water, and the dark line of the footbridge in a scene designated as "schön" (and even "abenteuerlich"). Indeed, it is discernible throughout these several paragraphs that the tone of ambivalence and ambiguity, for which the limestone formations have been one leitmotif, is in a phase of diminuendo. The flood is first perceived as marring the beauty of the scene, but then immediately reassessed as an additional embellishment. And, in the sequence of paragraphs depicting the actual leave-taking of the surveyor, he reacts with only sympathetic curiosity to being shown an additional but similarly impoverished area of the pastor's humble dwelling. This turn to the positive or at least to a redefinition of hitherto ambivalent imagery and perceptions leads in the next narratively distinct section to what appears to be a simple but still reasonably dramatic narrative climax and potential resolution of the thematic interplay of ego, initiative, and socialization.

There is one transitional paragraph before the surveyor finds himself alone again in the Steinkar, and it also conveys his trust in the essential worthiness of his friend, the poor pastor. He recalls his puzzlement at hearing footsteps on the second floor during his overnight sojourn at the parsonage, which were never commented upon by his host. But he consciously puts away any lingering doubts when he asserts, "allein ich ließ mich den Gedanken nicht weiter anfechten, und schritt vorwärts" (78). Which is exactly what Stifter then does with his linear narrative thread as he depicts the surveyor strolling down to the edge of the flooded meadow to survey the effects of the deluge. In the reader's mind, however, the unexplained footsteps must be shelved for future reference, and again a thematically significant foreshadowing is achieved with a single narrative stroke. The action quickly shifts in the following paragraph to the aforementioned "climax," which takes place along the river's temporarily extended perimeter. The scene is set when the surveyor describes a social phenomenon he has not encountered before. The reflective reaction this encounter engenders in him is obvious:

> . . . so erlebte ich plötzlich ein Schauspiel, . . . und bekam eine Gesellschaft, die mir bisher in dem Steinlande nicht zu Teil geworden war. Außer meinen Arbeitern, mit denen ich so bekannt war, . . . daß wir uns wechselweise wie Werkzeuge vorkommen mußten, hatte ich nur einige Menschen in meinem Gasthause, manchen Wanderer auf dem Wege und den armen Pfarrer in den Gesteinen gesehen. Jetzt sollte es anders werden. (78)

The surveyor watches attentively as a charming gaggle of local school children approaches the bridge; one by one they doff their shoes and stockings and step from the submerged end of the footbridge into the water. They appear from the narrator's vantage point as a broken line of black dots on the gleaming surface as they wade across the river towards him. Suddenly he perceives a larger black shape in midstream, which is none other than "der arme Pfarrer" himself. The cleric is standing, as it turns out, in a rather deep depression left recently when a local farmer removed an enormous boulder from the field at the river's edge. He makes sure none of the wading children come too close to the hidden danger and directs them calmly across to the higher ground. The surveyor chats companionably with the children as each one reaches his position and waits for the others. He hears that such exigencies are not infrequent for the children, and since they must cross the Zirder to reach their school they accept the risks and inconveniences with innocent equanimity. The pastor finally approaches with the last child and gives friendly thanks to his friend for rushing to his aid. The surveyor is taken aback by this unmerited gratitude: "Ich erschrak über diese Zumutung . . . " (82). The vigor of his reaction seems to indicate that along with his assumed approval of the pastor's initiative, there is some hesitancy in his mind as to his own perception of what he has witnessed. And although he both clarifies the misunderstanding and offers assurance that he was ready to help if needed, his perceptual ambivalence is heightened by the other problematical facts of the children's lives, which come out as he is chatting with them. In this process the apparent thematic resolution suggested by this dramatic scene is once again suspended in the interest of extending the narrative.[4]

But what then is the author's intent here, thematically speaking? The element of ego can no longer seriously be viewed as ambiguous in the pastor since he has clearly demonstrated an effective social interaction in his professionally localized capacity. His personal initiative is clearly successful, as none of the children were lost. The recurrent color motifs have also been arranged to display a "black and white" situation: the children are described as black dots approaching the larger black form of their benefactor as they traverse the gleaming current (79). Conspicuously lacking is the thematically important element of "gray." It seems once again confirmed, even before this ostensibly climactic passage has concluded, that Stifter is not artistically content with merely formulating in "Kalkstein" an alternative psychological frame of reference for evaluating the thematic interplay of ego, initiative, and socialization.[5] He is also intent upon constructing that frame of reference out of the other compositional and narrative elements which comprise this novella, residual ambivalances notwithstanding. Thus, he has oriented his narrative to its final direction. By leaving just enough perceptual ambiguity in the mind of the narrator regarding the pastor, Stifter now begins to establish that ambiguity as the salient and permanent feature of his thematic variation.

The surveyor bids the children and the pastor farewell after the river crossing, and they proceed on to morning mass and school while he climbs up the rocky slopes of what he now refers to as "meine Steine." This open reconciliation with the symbolic landscape is accompanied or perhaps occasioned by the distant pealing of bells which signal the morning mass "die der Pfarrer abhalten und der Kinder beiwohnen würden" (84). Psychologically the surveyor now sees himself as a part of the milieu, and significantly he goes "tiefer in die Steine hinein" to find his work crew. There follows here a narrative shift effected by a recapitulation and consolidation from the surveyor's viewpoint, one and a half pages in length, of the overall characterization which has been developed for the pastor. There are, as always, a few deceptively innocuous and seemingly incidental additional insights included, and the general tonal direction of the passage is clearly towards a reflective consideration of the truly problematical phenomenon of "dem armen

Pfarrer im Steinkar." This introspection was hinted at in the surveyor's ambivalence toward the rocky basin topography cited earlier and it now begins to focus on the character of the pastor. It will continue to develop, however, as their friendship solidifies, and it will remain the chief character trait of the surveyor in his function as narrative foil or witness to the gradual revelation of the pastor's essential character and the dilemma it creates. As will become apparent, this dilemma is not simply the failure of an eccentric ego to initiate a productive integration with mainstream society, but rather the assessment of that attempt by the witnesses to it, who are themselves drawn into the initiative by the integrity of the pastor. The surveyor assimilates and verifies features of the pastor's behavior and history from the hearsay and assertions of the locals. The information comes collectively "aus dem Munde der Menschen" (84). This open orientation towards the source of his information fits well with the surveyor's new reflective mood and contrasts with his earlier instinctive unwillingness to ask questions concerning his new acquaintance. He learns that the pastor's strange sleeping habits are a matter of public knowledge and that he rents his upper story to a pensioner and his daughter. It also comes to light that the pastor personally aids selected parishioners economically and that, due to the suspicion of hidden wealth accumulated through his austere life-style, he has been robbed several times. Structurally this latter fact, the first unequivocal designation of a failed initiative resulting from the pastor's egocentricity, comes near the end of the passage and contains a strong intimation of the practical nature which the narrative's ultimate depiction of personal initiative will have. But true to his narrative techniques of balance and in keeping with his exposition of the evaluative dilemma now central to the plot, Stifter immediately terminates the passage with unqualifiedly positive but still reflective images of his main character. Although the pastor himself will later openly admit his problematical position, it is thematically important that it is the surveyor who first alludes to the evaluative dilemma which is still gradually emerging. For it is this dilemma which is the key to realizing the underlying thematic variation in "Kalkstein":

> Ich konnte von diesen Dingen weder wissen was wahr sei, noch was nicht wahr sei. So oft ich zu ihm kam, sah ich die ruhigen klaren blauen Augen, das einfache Wesen und die bittere ungeheuchelte Armut. Was seine Vergangenheit gewesen sei, in das drang ich nicht ein, und mochte nicht eindringen. (85)

Ironically, but not unexpectedly, Stifter will devote most of the latter part of the novella to an exposition of this "past." First, however, he interposes a pair of medium-length paragraphs which center upon the character of the surveyor alone, in his professional role as a government employee.

There at first appears to be a regression in his character in this passage, as the surveyor once again becomes preoccupied with patently negative aspects of the stoney basin land, or Steinkar. He refers to the troublesome boulder masses ["Steinnester"] of those inhospitable landscapes ["unwirtlichen Landschaften"] which present so many hindrances ["Hindernisse"] to his efforts, and he compares the area unfavorably with "einer gezähmten und fruchtbaren Gegend," such as the Schauendorf region perhaps (86). This apparent inconsistency in the outlook of the narrator revolves around his own sudden confrontation with the possibility of a failed personal initiative and the crucial evaluative factor of "time" is at the heart of his crisis. The authorities have issued a time limit for his work and have already assigned him his next, distantly located project. He reacts with a frustration borne of professional pressures and his new, almost subconscious attachment to the "Steinland." After disparaging anew the natural features of the basin landscape, he ironically decides to resolve his dilemma by leaving his haven in the Hochstraße and descending permanently to the work site, where he even recruits more locals to finish the surveying. The novelty of his predicament is indicated by his desperation to avoid the shame of missing a deadline, and his ego-centered pride in skillfully completing a difficult task has him up nights recopying his drawings and maps to perfection (86). There is, of course, a narrative logic in submersing the surveyor in his own activities in order to provide a context for the time lapse which now occurs in his central relationship with the pastor. But the thematic interplay of ego, initiative, and socialization never seems completely lost from sight as the surveyor acts out his own duplicative version of it in these two paragraphs. It should be remembered that his evaluation of the pastor's resolution of the three thematic elements will form the contextual format for expressing the variation of their interplay presented in "Kalkstein." To have the pastor's characterizational foil, the surveyor, too explicitly or too readily adopt the pastor's mannerisms or methods would reduce the total thematic to a simple didactic exposition. Such simplicity seldom occurs in Stifter's writing, even when it appears to; and the irony present in the opening line of the next paragraph in "Kalkstein" is a reintroduction of the principal narrative strand.

The surveyor uses his professional preoccupation to explain his neglect of his new friendship: "Daß mir bei diesen Arbeiten der Pfarrer in den Hintergrund trat ist begreiflich" (86). But his ever-growing psychological bond with the cleric is evident in the use of the color motif to reintroduce their relationship. The surveyor expresses his state of mind as being restless ["unruhig"], when he realizes the pastor has desisted for some time from his customary wanderings among the limestone. He has been "gewöhnt seine schwarze Gestalt in den Steinen zu sehen, . . . weil er der einzige dunkle Punkt in der graulich dämmernden . . . Kalkflur war" (87). In his own professional dilemma, the surveyor senses that the pastor in his professional capacity has somehow dealt with the ambiguities and problems represented by the rocky landscape. He ascertains that his friend has been ill and utilizes, or more exactly ["oder vielmehr"], creates an opportunity to visit him. The old pastor's situation at this point is almost the reverse of the surveyor's. Whereas the surveyor has been drawn out of his objective stance toward the basin landscape and its inhabitants and pressured by the dictates of his personal initiative into a physical proximity and social interaction with them, the pastor has been removed from his usual sphere of activity even to the point of having to occupy the conventional sleeping accommodations previously reserved for his guests. This reversal of orientations, besides enhancing the sublimative process of the dual-characterization, also provides a logical narrative premise for the following major segment of the novella: the pastor's autobiographical story-within-a-story. Up to this point he has been consistently depicted as a person of calm wisdom and few words. He is now about to embark on a monologue which will cover some fifty-plus years of his life and some twenty full pages of text. The pretext for such uncharacteristic loquacity is his stay in bed due to an extended illness, but an important development of the thematic interplay can be expected now, commensurate with such a lengthy interpolation. The emphasis, however, will once again be upon the ego component of the three-way thematic interaction—this time in a developmentally analytical direction. There will be varied instances of personal initiative and a generally conventional socialization centered on home and family to support and highlight this intensification of analysis of the work's central figure. The narrative direction here is not contradictory to the earlier assertion in this chapter that the essentially legitimate outlines of the protagonist's personality are largely established in the surveyor's mind after the river crossing scene. Rather, it is in support of the likewise asserted view that the narrative's thematic focus would begin to narrow to the problematic evaluation of the parson's final initiative at resolving his apparent egocentricity in a socially productive manner. By the end of the autobiographical sketch, the inevitability and, hence, thought provoking complexity of his dilemma will be evident. The final thematic phase of the novella, the poor pastor's final initiative and the assessment of its success or failure from a social viewpoint, will then begin.

Stifter leads into the inner narrative with a series of prefatory paragraphs which reestablish stylistically, structurally, and contextually several of his earlier motifs concerning the pastor, the surveyor and the social backdrop for their relationship. The two men greet each other cordially, but their exchange is reported for the most part in the subjunctive mood, reevoking the friendly but almost shy formality of their earlier meetings. Even the now demysticized egocentricity and highly individualized psychological orientation of the cleric appears revived in the image of his placid but firm refusal to receive any medical ministrations. His behavior stems from the strange reasoning ["seltsamen Grund"] that medicine is "eine Versuchung Gottes" (87). The surveyor's attachment to the outside world, which has been a salient feature in his role as characterizational foil, is echoed in his journey by postillion to a doctor in a nearby city to get an opinion on the pastor's chances for recovery (88). This reemergence of general character traits seems to be motivated in part by the author's need to recreate at least enough narrative suspense to bring the reader's full attention to bear upon the numerous narrative details in the pastor's self-portrait and upon their thematic implications. As regards the surveyor, his evaluative orientation will remain in the reader's consciousness, as a constant point of reference for the gradually emerging thematic dilemma.

The pastor's immediate personal society is suddenly expanded not only by an intensification of involvement with his few usual companions, but also by the presence of several hitherto incidental characters. The surveyor and Sabine, the pastor's elderly part-time housekeeper, make daily visits in spite of their own busy schedules, and two fellow clerics from neighboring parishes drop in along with the schoolmaster from the Steinkar. Most interesting is the priest's reaction to the visits of his pensioner's lovely young daughter, whose presence causes him to shyly pull the covers up around his chin. Thus the important "linen" motif is reevoked in preparation for its general explication forthcoming in the story-within-a-story. It should also be realized that this is only the third and, as it turns out, the final scene of the main narrative in which the pastor is depicted in a social context with more than one other character. The first such scene was his visit to the church celebration in Schauendorf which served primarily to introduce and delineate his eccentric appearance and potentially egocentric personality. The second was the scene with the children in the Zirder which, in its turn, practically resolved his ambiguous character traits in a positive manner. The third social scenario then, reviving as it does several ambivalent aspects of the early characterization of the pastor and at least one still unclarified leitmotif (the linens), creates a need for further thematic resolution. Also, the increasingly socialized contexts of the narrative situations clearly suggest that this coming resolution will center around an evaluation of the protagonist's integration into society. Stifter continues to highlight the social element of the thematic interplay of ego, initiative, and socialization in the final passages of the preautobiographical narrative by depicting how the pastor becomes much more open and talkative with his surveyor friend. He grows accustomed to hearing articles read to him from newspapers brought in from the outside world, and he also receives further instruction in the whys and wherefores of surveying from his friend. Another important element of characterization is being developed or sublimated in these images: the highly individualistic personality of the pastor is gradually being attuned to a broader social outlook than he has previously been willing to consider. The process is balanced as always. He has elicited by passive attention at least the surveyor's worldly knowledge of professional and social life; yet, he also insists that the surveyor tell him about all the natural activities taking place out in the rocky landscape, from the ripening of the blackberries and hawthorn down to the pace of the geological weathering of the limestone (89). This further example of a role reversal between the pastor and his foil supports the earlier stated view that Stifter's thematic intent is not that either of his two major figures should psychologically convert to the orientation of the other. It is now the pastor's turn to demonstrate enough insight into his companion's more conventional frame of reference to bring the problematical evaluative aspect of the thematic variation to the narrative forefront. The pastor can certainly not be accused of any attempt at ingratiation in this context, even though he informs the surveyor a few lines after the depiction of their new comraderie, "er hatte eine Bitte an ihn." He remains consistent in his characteristic independence as evidenced by the gratitude he expresses to the surveyor for his trip to the city doctor just a few paragraphs after he has declared his general distrust of physicians as a whole (cf. 87). The pastor's final words to the surveyor before he begins his lengthy biographical revelations signal an attempt at explication and analysis and alert the reader that evaluation will be necessary:

> Ich muß Ihnen, ehe ich meine Bitte ausspreche, erst etwas erzählen. Bemerken Sie wohl, ich erzähle es nicht, weil es wichtig ist, sondern, damit Sie sehen, wie alles so gekommen ist, was jetzt ist, und damit sie viel geneigter werden, meine Bitte zu erfüllen. Sie sind immer sehr gut gegen mich gewesen . . . . Dies gibt mir nun den Mut, mich an Sie zu wenden. (90)

As befits the plain demeanor of the person who utters it, the pastor's autobiographical digression is structurally and stylistically characterized by paragraphs of fairly uniform length and chronologically arranged content, by vivid, but unadorned imagery and descriptions, and by intentionally unexceptional grammatical phrasing and word choice. There are, for example, very few subjunctive constructions in comparison to the frequent and often seemingly pointed use of that form earlier in the novella. The details given of the pastor's family history, childhood, and young adulthood are also fairly uncomplicated in summary: he was one of twin scions of a successful line of tanners, and he always lagged behind his sibling in academic and business aptitude. He was frustrated in his first and only romantic relationship and, subsequent to the sudden loss of the family business and fortune, he buried his brother and entered the priesthood. He received his parish after several years assisting other pastors, and has for many years since been pursuing his duties and unusual way of life in the Steinland. Within this schematic outline, however, Stifter has created a quietly powerful depiction of a forming ego inescapably affected by its hereditary and environmental expectations. The author devotes one each of the first three, equally developed paragraphs to the three immediate forebears of the poor pastor. The great-grandfather, the founder of the line, is a foundling from the far away region of Swabia (90). Stifter has posited here a starting point for the development of his protagonist which has no previous societal reference point. When the great-grandfather is described as wandering into the city with his walking stick, the image is very reminiscent of that of the pastor at the consecration celebration. The wanderer's background is similarly vague, and he is, to all appearances, an *Einzelgänger* with a hint of the eccentric or at least of the unfamiliar about him. But, the great-grandfather's social orientation turns out to be the opposite of his descendant's and more like the character of the surveyor in that earlier scene. He is depicted as entering, not leaving, a social context and he applies his personal initiative among charitable folk from whom he learns his trade (90). After his journeyman travels and a stint as foreman, he marries a poor girl and starts his own tannery. Thematically, this figure clearly provides a model for successful social integration of a distinctive ego by productive initiative. His socialization is vouched for by his reputation at his death "als ein geachteter bei den Geschäftsleuten angesehener Mann" (90). Yet, the isolation of his ego, though intentionally understated, is maintained by his desire to operate "als eigener Herr sein Gewerbe und seine Handelschaft" (90). It seems clear from the long series of "er" clauses, and from the single passing reference to a wife, that his personal initiatives are to preserve a basically egocentric character. This pattern of understated egoism continues for the grandfather and father figures as well. They are only sons who consolidate and extend the social integration of their strong individual personalities through productive personal initiatives. Again, the "distaff" contribution to the family ascension is downplayed in the interest of enhancing the thematic element of ego manifest in the father-to-son progression. A grandmother is not mentioned at all, and the pastor's own mother is quickly dispensed with as having died in childbirth. But Stifter doesn't abandon his structural and narrative techniques of foreshadowing and overlapping even in this systematically composed biographical interpolation. The lack of a personal love relationship, which is formalized in the character of the widowed father, sets a pattern of solitude which will be very significant in the pastor's own situation.

As stated above, the father figure has his own paragraph depicting his particular approach to the ongoing resolution of the universal interplay of ego, initiative, and socialization (91). But in contrast with the other progenitors, there are signs in his actions of a different focus on the ego element of the interplay from a more private, subjective viewpoint. Whereas the ego-initiated socialization effected by the two earlier forebears was translated in general terms of business success and social prestige, the process seems to have reached a level with the father which allows, or perhaps even elicits, more consciously personalized attitudes and actions. He does continue the expansion of the family fortunes, but these initiatives are recalled from the living memory of his son and not recited schematically from a family history. The pastor even recalls the large black dog, Hassan, who guarded the family courtyard. As if to finalize this thematically important "resubjectivization," Stifter grants the father an additional paragraph in which his non-business activities are cited, such as his love of orchard husbandry and his habit of personally administering medicine to his sick employees. These last two images are strongly reminiscent of the poor pastor's clerical colleagues in the outer narrative whose sensible actions often seem to contrast with his own. With the father figure, the author continues the imaginal progression from a mechanistic and merchantile-based socialization, through more private but still essentially productive initiatives, to patently ego-centered self-conscious surface manifestations of proper social integration. The last descriptive detail devoted to the father as an independent character in the story states: "Dem Prunke war er abgeneigt, daß er eher zu schlicht und unscheinbar daher ging als zu ansehnlich, seine Wohnung war einfach, und wenn er in einem Wagen ausfuhr, so mußte es ein sehr bürgerlich aussehender sein" (92). Having thus introduced into the biography the first intimation of problematic eccentricity and its potential for the three-part thematic interplay, Stifter creates a narrative point of departure for more of the same by complicating the heretofore unilinear succession of the family line: twin sons are born.

In the delineation of the pastor's family tree there is an implied contrastive pairing of the eccentric cleric with each of his three forebears. This contrast concludes significantly with a problematic egocentrism in the characterization of the father, similar to that manifested in the outer narrative in the pastor's own character. But when the death of the aging, increasingly reclusive sire is described shortly thereafter in the text, it is clear that the full development of this thematically central problem will be constructed around the relationship between the twin brothers. The funeral of the father is presented in images which acknowledge his successful, but still personal resolution of the interplay of ego, initiative, and socialization:

> Mit seinem Leichenzuge gingen alle Armen der Stadtbezirkes, es gingen die Männer seines Geschäftes mit seine Freunde viele Fremde, die Arbeiter seines Hauses und seine zwei Söhne. Es wurden sehr viele Tränen geweint, wie man um wenig Menschen des Landes weint, und die Leute sagten daß ein

vortrefflicher Mann ein auserlesener Bürger und ein ehrenvoller Geschäftsmann begraben worden sei. (99)

As he has earlier in the story, Stifter continues the ongoing thematic development with the pairing of characters. The brothers, although identical in appearance and background, exhibit from the first almost opposite configurations of mental gifts ["Geistesgaben"]. The pastor is always the hindmost in their schooling and apprenticeship, even to the point of failing the state school examinations and proving himself inadequate to participate constructively in the family business. But while he is demonstrating this early inability to express his individual ego through conventionally acceptable social initiatives, that same ego is being portrayed in increasingly sympathetic, even lovable terms. He is a favorite with the tannery workers because of his cheerful willingness to run errands. Even the family tutor is genuinely affectionate towards his diligent but hapless student. It is the twin brother himself, however, who most clearly serves as a foil for the pastor's increasingly sympathetic characterization.

The more able and, hence, more overtly socialized sibling has taken on an ever larger share in administering the family business as his father has retreated more and more to his garden and orchards. He agrees that his brother can return to their long since vacated nursery in order to reapply himself to his failed studies. The thematic significance of this situation seems clear: the pastor, motivated by his sympathetic but essentially eccentric psychological make-up, pursues an autodidatic endeavor while his brother immerses himself completely in the conventional social mainstream of commerce. Stifter, however, does not often offer overtly simplistic characterizations, even for his auxiliary figures. So it soon becomes apparent that the complex of ego, initiative, and socialization represented in the single character of the father is to be dichotomized by and, fascinatingly enough, also within the personalities and fates of both brothers. When the ownership of the tannery finally passes officially to the twin heirs, the pastor is quite willing to apply his newly acquired but still incomplete educational skills to helping his brother administer the business. There is almost an element of personal pique in the twin's sensible explanation that the business could well founder waiting for his brother's level of reeducation to become commensurate with the responsibility of a full partnership (100). But the competent twin promises at the same time that he will apply himself totally to the preservation of the family welfare. He leaves the question open, with no discernible sense of resentment, as to what part his brother will play in their future. The future pastor heeds his brother's realistic appraisal and returns to the tacitly egocentric pursuit of his studies. The twin brother's own developing psychological one-sideness is reflected in his single-minded devotion to the legal aspects of their co-inheritance, in ironic contrast to his own suggestion that his brother should seek a broad-based course of study and certification in preparation for a professional career.

The essentially positive but socially isolated ego of the future pastor leaps up at the suggestion of having an identifiable profession, a socially established and condoned pattern for personal initiative. He applies himself with eager energy to his studies and begins to accumulate official certifications of his achievements. The next natural step in his quest for meaningful social integration would be to form a personal union, a love relationship, from which traditional base a further modification and integration of the individual personality would enhance his personal initiatives. And he does manage to meet and, in his own naive and guileless manner, to court a pretty young neighbor girl whose mother operates a laundry for fine linens on the property adjacent to the tannery and estate. The natural sociability of this union is simply expressed in the pastor's own recollection of it: "Zuletzt kamen wir auch zum Sprechen. Was wir gesprochen haben, weiß ich nicht mehr. Es muß gewöhnliches Ding gewesen sein. Wir nahmen uns auch bei den Händen" (104).[6] But both of the young people have intuited from their home environments the need for some outward, conventionally recognizable symbol of socialization in regard to all important initiatives, even very personal ones. The pastor has his dreams of a professional identity and the girl has been taught that expensive linen and other domestic finery represent the acme of individualized social integration (105). The pastor quickly assimilates his beloved's viewpoint, seeing it perhaps as a wonderfully personalized seal for their youthfully idealized outlooks. The young man begins henceforth to acquire linens and silver for the future, and the key to understanding the linen motif of the main narrative is finally revealed when he remarks of his beloved: "Ich erinnerte mich... daß ich an dem Körper... immer am Rande des Halses oder an dem Ärmeln die feinste weiße Wäsche gesehen hatte..." (105). Having thus poised his protagonist on the brink of a final non-problematical and conventional resolution of the interplay of ego, initiative, and socialization, Stifter reorients the narrative context towards the failure of that resolution for an eccentric personality.

The figure of the competent twin brother, the partner in the biographical conundrum created in these passages, is reintroduced as the financial agency enabling the pastor to pursue his quest for the personal effects ["Geräte"] of happiness. But the brother is meant to share in the unhappy conclusion of this story-within-the-story and he must later face the consequences of his own unequal ablities and talents ["Geistesgaben"] when the family business collapses. First though, his shy twin is forcefully parted from his sweetheart by the disapproval of her mother. This lady seems to represent a type of ego-centric social initiative which has been materially oriented to the point of dehumanization. Or one could perhaps fault the pastor for not having enough practical social skills to effectively implement his desires in a conventionally acceptable way. He is, after all, at this point still the co-owner of a business and has an allowance sufficient to purchase household fineries. One can only surmise what might have transpired had he made those purchases with the knowledge and advice of his potential mother-in-law. Needless to say, such a scenario has no place in Stifter's artistic and thematic intentions for "Kalkstein." He juxtaposes the failures of the two brothers, one after the other, to finalize the image of the poor pastor as heir to a sympathetic personality, but one unable to reconcile ego and society in conventional ways. The youth responds touchingly in an intuited recognition of his personal isolation when he learns that his girl has been married off to a distant kinsman. He declares, "Ich meinte damals, daß ich mir die Seele aus dem Körper weinen müsse" (106). The use of the subjunctive reminds the reader of the strength of character which has enabled the protagonist to overcome difficulty and which continues as one element in the complex of self and society created by the main narrative. Ironically, the twin brother with his devotion to business could probably have managed the practical aspects of initiating a formal engagement of his own, but he has had no time for such personal initiatives. This lack of a more substantial familial relationship may be in part responsible for the public loss of financial confidence in the tannery which leads quickly to a run on assets and the irreversible collapse of the business. The brother dies from the trauma of his failure, and included in his obituary is the pointed remark that he was "unverheiratet" (107). There is also a blatant contrast in the paucity of mourners at the twin's funeral compared with the universal mourning at his father's interment. The implication seems to be that each of the twin brothers was doomed by circumstances to develop only one aspect of a normal ego, thus limiting the nature and success of their initiatives toward social integration. The pastor by dint of his self-constructed isolation has developed a gentle but basically egocentric strength, which simultaneously preserves him from destructive personal trauma while it limits his practical success in social contexts. His brother, contrastively, has had no opportunity to develop the inner self; and in spite of his systematic acumen in business affairs, he does not possess the inner strength to survive a major setback in those affairs .

At this point the complex characterization of the story's main figure is basically complete. The pastor returns to the main narrative after describing how he liquidated the family assets in order to satisfy the creditors and preserve the integrity of the family name. There is some irony in the fact that there is no family to bear this name, as the pastor then seeks the anonymity of the seminary. His altruistic but basically anticlimactic effort also points toward the image of the pastor to be presented in the context of his final initiative: an essentially positive personality whose only models for socially productive initiatives have been in financial and legal contexts, both antithetical to his natural psychology and removed from the normal sphere of his chosen vocation. The pastor's logical but nonetheless subjunctively expressed and inhibited ["beklemmt"] decision to seek ordination reaffirms the basically humanistic nature of his personal dilemma. It is also revealing that only two lines of text are devoted to his religious training period in comparison to the lengthy passages describing his earlier, secular efforts (108). He is so sensitive to the possibility of professional jealousy that he accepts only a parish no one else wants and then only after there can be no accusations of premature advancement. His determination to subordinate himself to the interest of others, ironically, places him in an increasingly egocentric position. And just as the bridge over the Zirder often fails in its function of securing the way into the basin land, so too, the pastor confesses to his surveyor friend, have his previous efforts to help his community often failed. He has been officially censured twice for renting his upper story and robbers have thrice taken his savings intended for public aid. At this point in the pastor's monologue, there is some thematic suspense produced by his admission of wise investments in orphans' insurance after the robberies. But considering his problematic psychology and advanced age, one suspects this endeavor will ultimately be but one more insufficient attempt at altruistic service. His request of the surveyor to keep one of three legal copies of his will takes on an extra significance in this context. How logically superficial this request will really be seems subtly anticipated by the pastor's continuing confession when he admits that he cannot part with the fine linen he has worn for years in memory of his lost love. The true substance and outcome of his final request is ironically foreshadowed in his belief that: "Nach meinem Tode wird sie ja auch etwas eintragen" (109). The author will leave the revelation of the pastor's final testament, or initiative as it were, till the final passages of the novella. Thematically this climax will give full perceptual force to the problematical variation in "Kalkstein" of the ego-initiative-socialization dynamic which pervades *Bunte Steine* as a whole.

In advance of this climax, Stifter focuses once again on the viewpoint of the surveyor/narrator, who will be called upon to evaluate the pastor's final initiative. After the ritualized signing and exchanging of documents pursuant to his custody of the third will, the surveyor prepares for and takes his leave from the Steingegend amid images which connote his perception of a final reconciliation of the thematic elements in the person, life, and endeavors of his friend. He states: "Wie aber alles ein Ende nimmt, so war es auch mit unserem langen Aufenthalt im Steinkar" (112). He bids adieu to the pastor and several others in the same sentence but in two separate phrases, as if to hint at an only tentative integration for the cleric. This tentativeness is underscored by his reference to the symbolic landscape as being now free of those who sought to catalogue and classify its enigmatic uniqueness. His own growing insight into the complex nature of the pastor's position has assumed deeply emotional dimensions by the time he mounts the departing postillion:

> Eines sehr seltsamen Gefühles muß ich Erwähnung tun . . . . Es ergriff mich nämlich beinahe eine tiefe Wehmut, als ich von der Gegend schied . . . . Wie ich immer mehr und mehr in die bewohnteren Teile hinauskam, mußte ich . . . nach den Steinen zurückschauen, deren Lichter so sanft und matt schimmerten, und in deren Vertiefungen die schönen blauen Schatten waren . . . (113)

The ambiguous grayness of the region has yielded to the mysterious serenity of deep, blue shadows and shimmering lights, but many years will pass before the surveyor returns to consciously experience the thematic revelations they anticipate. (A brief visit he does make some five years later (114) only reaffirms the temporary nature of the narrative resolution seemingly present in his first farewell to the pastor. He cites the unchanging scene, including significantly the inn on the Hochstraße as part of the general imaginal amalgam.)

The narrator fills the passing years with work which coincidentally never brings him back to the river basin community. But he does correspond regularly with his former companion, and when the old priest finally passes away the surveyor journeys to his burial with almost filial self-reproach for his imagined neglect. The final exposition of the pastor's highly problematical attempt at resolving the tension between his unique ego, his initiatives, and his impulse toward socialization is now to be narratively worked out through the content of his last will and testament. The surveyor, as if gathering last insights and girding himself psychologically for the evaluative dilemma which will fall to him, revisits the parsonage, the inn on the Hochstraße, and the unchanged rocky barrens, while he awaits the final reading of the will. He also reflects on the last days of the cleric (as related to him at the funeral), during which the old man uncharacteristically allowed the conventional ministration of medicine but only after the final sacrament. The large crowd at the burial is affectionately bereaved and this suggests a comparison with the funerals of both his father and brother. But there is also a large element of curiosity in the crowd, once again pointing up the eccentric aspects of the pastor's character. Significantly the pensioner's daughter, the living metaphor for the pastor's lost personal life, was not with him at the end (116). With this final picture of the poor pastor of the Steinkar (with its almost Christlike combination of self-sacrificing goodness and profound psychological isolation) in his memory, the surveyor becomes privy to and must evaluate his friend's final initiative.

The will is processed according to the rituals of the conventional society with which the pastor sought to integrate himself throughout his lonely life, as far as his pure but essentially egocentric nature would permit. And, although quite believable in regard to the society present at the hearing, there is irony for the reader in the surveyor's assertion that: "Der Inhalt des Testamentes aber überraschte alle" (117). The contents outline in simple, sincere language the pastor's plan to contribute the entire worth of his estate to building a second schoolhouse on the far side of the Zirder, thus eliminating the dangers to the Steingegend children posed by the erratic rise and fall of the waters. There is also provision for the new teacher's lodging and salary, as well as for a fair recompense for the teacher on the other side of the basin whose enrollment and income would be consequently affected. There is also contained within the will a brief description in the first person of the pastor's trials and tribulations prior to and subsequent to conceiving and implementing his plan. Although modestly phrased, this appendix-like confession appears to be included by Stifter to give one final positive highlight to his main character before passing on to the final thematic statement expressed in the narrator's evaluation. The personally mandated auction of the pastor's effects follows, and it is significant that all his humble belongings are purchased—even a tattered coat brings a generous price from a fellow cleric. The surveyor purchases the entire collection of fine linens and the beautiful crucifix, both relics from a time when the protagonist held all the normal expectations for a happy, productive life. The surveyor states that these linens are to be preserved by him and his wife as a monument to the pastor's lost dreams, just as they were kept during his lifetime. In fact, all the sincere albeit tardy homage to the deceased that is manifest in this auction scene is directed at the humanly sympathetic aspects of the pastor's character which have been his personal trademark since his youth. What then is the worth in social terms of this problematically unique ego's final initiative? Or, as the surveyor so succinctly puts it: "Nun stellt sich die Frage, was die Wirkung von all diesen Dingen gewesen sei" (121). The subjunctive mode, used one last time here, seems to anticipate the irony of the surveyor/narrator's final attempt at a conventional understanding of his friend's apparent failure within the society he took as his own many years before. The monetary tally falls far short of that needed to implement the pastor's last wishes. Hence, the humanistic and religious elements of his opinion are both no doubt sincere when the surveyor solemnly declares: " Es lag das in der Natur des Pfarrers, der die Weltdinge nicht verstand . . .", and then adds:

> Aber wie das Böse stets in sich selber zwecklos ist, und im Weltplane keine Wirkung hat, das Gute aber Früchte trägt, wenn es auch mit mangelhaften Mitteln begonnen wird, so war es auch hier: Gott bedurfte zur Krönung dieses Werkes des Pfarrers nicht. (121)

Although the agency of belated success for the pastor's final initiative takes the form of a subscription by the well-to-do and rich of the area to achieve the goals set forth in his testament, the final thematic statement for "Kalkstein" is solemnly implied in the last paragraph of the work. The narrator, who at this point seems barely separable from the author himself, says:

> Das einzige Kreuz, das für einen Pfarrer in dem Kirchhofe des Kar steht, steht auf dem Hügel des Gründers dieser Dinge. Es mag manchmal ein Gebet dabei verrichtet werden, und mancher wird mit einem Gefühle davor stehen, das dem Pfarrer nicht gewidmet worden ist, da er noch lebte. (122)

"Der arme Pfarrer im Kar" has shown his friend, and all sensitive souls who may reflect on his story, that the universal human struggle to socialize the individual ego through constructive initiative is sometimes not reducible to the conventional criteria of success or failure. This solitary figure with his simple but profound communion with the human heart is not to be judged on the practical results of his own inadequate, ego-generated attempts at social integration, but rather on the willingness his struggle motivates in others to participate individually in the collective social welfare.[7] In conclusion, it has been attempted in this chapter to demonstrate that a three-way interplay of ego, initiative, and socialization is the dominant thematic complex for the second novella of Adalbert Stifter's *Bunte Steine* as it was for the first. It has also been seen that in spite of several structural and stylistic similarities, such as the continued use of reiterative and duplicative compositional techniques to produce narrative suspense and fullness, "Kalkstein" exhibits basic dissimilarities with "Granit," its antecedent in the collection. The most significant of these differences in the creation of a thematic variation are the use of an extended, two-pronged characterization and a linear narrative flow involving only one major character and his narrative foil.

It will be the task of the next chapter of this study to consider what reciprocal compositional and thematic variations the author may effect in the last specimen from his *Bunte Steine* chosen for analysis. "Katzensilber," unlike granite or limestone, is fit neither for foundations nor sculpture—it is a natural curiosity, whose chief function is to beguile the attention and imagination of its beholder.

NOTES

1. Konrad seems correct, at least in this particular context, that for Stifter "Religion war ihm nur ein Mittel zu Sittlichkeit." See Konrad 367.
2. It should be noted here that the text used for this study, the 1963 edition by Max Stefl, states on page four, "Die Zeichensetzung entspricht der der Erstdrucke; ebenso wurden gewisse Eigenheiten der Stifter'schen Rechtschreibung beibehalten."
3. Konrad Steffen implies the mastery of this technique came late to Stifter, but rightly perceives it as "die rechte Spannung" for the attentive reader. See Steffen 27.
4. Blackall's assessment of this passage as "the central episode in 'Kalkstein'" does not seenm to give full credit to the thematic connection of all that precedes and follows it. See Blackall 263.
5. Were the story to end here, Bleckwenn's view of Stifter's use of "der erzählerische Trick der Umwertung" might be more justified. See Bleckwenn 112.
6. The charming, uncomplicated compatibility depicted here doesn't quite fit Aluf's pronouncement that in Stifter's work love represents a quest for what one lacks in oneself. See Aluf 21.
7. This is a significantly deeper concept than the simple posthumous integration of an "Außenseiter." See Bleckwenn 108.

Chapter IV

"Katzensilber"

THERE ARE TWO MAJOR REASONS for selecting "Katzensilber" as the third and final novella from *Bunte Steine* to be considered in this study. First, Stifter's often gripping and moving story of a mountain girl of unclear, apparently Gypsy origins and her ultimately tragic interaction with a prosperous Austrian farm family expresses in simple, straightforward characterization and narrative the tripartite thematic interplay of ego, initiative, and socialization. Secondly, the particular variation of this universal dynamic expressed in "Katzensilber" is as topical today as it must have been in Stifter's time. The view here appears to be that the three-way interplay while essentially positive is nonetheless demarcated by material and psychological "limits." These limits provide a structured format for fulfillment but, at the same time, they leave open the suspenseful possibility of conflict with some other equally positive but culturally antithetical format governing the same dynamic.

Of the six novellas contained in *Bunte Steine*, only this one was written specifically for the collection. The other five works all appeared in earlier, sometimes significantly different versions. The question of an identifiable "development" must necessarily arise whenever a series of literary works by a single author is considered. "Katzensilber" would indeed be the logical point of departure for a separate monograph on the possibility of a thematic development or maturation within *Bunte Steine*, given the unique inceptional relationship of this particular novella to the collection as a whole. However, such an endeavor would require a detailed comparison and contrast of the thematic aspects of all of the extant versions of all six of the novellas. This would exceed the time and space limits of the present study but could certainly be a complementary project for the future. For now, it must suffice that those developmental aspects which seem apparent in the thematic variation expressed in "Katzensilber" will serve primarily as adjuncts to demonstrating the relationship between that variation and the respective variations found in "Granit" and "Kalkstein."

From a textual analysis of "Katzensilber" similar to those undertaken above for "Granit" and "Kalkstein," it can be suggested that Stifter again utilizes the same general compositional techniques present in the latter two works to maintain the omnipresence of his thematic interplay and to suspend any premature narrational resolution of it. These techniques include the juxtaposition of contextually, structurally, and imaginally duplicative passages, highly connotative word choice, and the thematically purposive use of particular grammatical modalities. The textual analysis should likewise reveal some differences peculiar to "Katzensilber" in the balance, emphasis, and quantitative ratio of these compositional elements. There is, for example, a notably more sparing use of the subjunctive and a proportionate increase in the use of impersonal constructions using "man" and "lassen." There is also a notable reduction in the use of the frame or "Rahmen" technique, which accommodates only a few parabolic insertions one or two pages in length or less. Just as the collective working of compositional and thematic interaction produces an overall narrative direction of circular consolidation for "Granit" and one of linear clarification for "Kalkstein," it will be seen to create a vertical narrative axis for "Katzensilber." Up and down the length of this axis will be worked out the thematic variation of two positive but ultimately exclusive formats of human socialization narratively juxtaposed and brought into suspenseful contact. The firm granite foundation of ego, initiative, and socialization established by Stifter in his first story in an autobiographical context and then varied as an individualized limestone monument in his second is to be symbolized in "Katzensilber" by a material which shines brightest in the environs of its particular natural setting. But far from being a retreat by the author from a conviction of the universality of his thematic interplay, "Katzensilber" represents a balanced combination of the best aspects of the two other works which supports his basic premise. "Katzensilber" possesses the philosophical breadth of "Granit" as well as the dramatically individualized focus of "Kalkstein."

The thematic component of initiative within this particular story achieves its crucial narrational development in the actions and reactions of the brown girl ["das braune Mädchen"], a consistently altruistic character whose connections to any clear segment of society are kept intentionally enigmatic. She is depicted as being practically without geographical, familial, or religious affiliations; and her exposure to these facets of socialization, in a form alien to her, constitutes the core of the thematic interplay in "Katzensilber" as well as a good deal of the narrative action. But there is more text devoted to characterizing the novella's other chief figures and to establishing the essential positivity of the conventionally socialized milieu of the story. In fact, the brown girl—thematically the work's central figure—does not appear until some fifteen pages, or approximately one fifth of the way into the text. Hence, one could speak of a narrative "preface" in the manner of those present in "Granit" and "Kalkstein." Such a comparison, however, reveals some apparent structural and contextual dissimilarities. The few preparatory passages in "Granit" serve to express the thematic interplay as a narrative springboard as it were, for the story of an as yet childish ego embarking upon a process of socialization. The more artistically contrived but equally brief psychological preface in "Kalkstein" previews the thematic variation to be expressed and initiates the consequent narrative tension. The first fifteen pages of "Katzensilber," by contrast, provide an openly positive, unproblematic description of a hill country farmstead ["Hof"] and its inhabitants and of the upper topographical limits of its activities. Even the style of the first segment of the work reveals a contrastively more objective and artistically distanced approach. The first person structures of the opening passages of "Granit" are here replaced by a preponderance of impersonal constructions with "man" and "lassen." Hence, the underlying tension of ego-versus-society is replaced by the image of an amalgam of self and society in the form of generalized and productive agrarian life and initiatives. The introductory section of "Kalkstein," while perhaps more similar to that of "Katzensilber" in a superficial way with its pseudo-objective philosophical pronouncements, is likewise quite dissimilar in its overt attempt at conditioning the reader's empathy in advance of the narrative.

As one continues to analyze "Katzensilber," it becomes apparent that the much more gradual introduction of the thematic variation of the ego, initiative, and socialization interplay expressed in this work derives from the nature of that variation. As mentioned above, another structural difference between "Katzensilber" and the other two novellas included in this study is the handling of the inner narrative, or the *Binnenerzählung*. In contrast to the substantial use of the story-within-a-story in both "Granit" and "Kalkstein," Stifter makes relatively little use of it in "Katzensilber," which is nonetheless the longest novella in *Bunte Steine*. With minimal exceptions these "tales" are contained within the first fifteen pages of the text, although the content of these anecdotal, parable-like stories actually holds the key not only to the novella's thematic variation but also to the overall relationship between that variation and the structural form of the work.

The most important of these tales, given in the form of stories told the farm children by their grandmother during excursions to the heights of the "Nußberg" ["nut mountain"], all depict the essentially negative results of interaction by the locals with beings from beyond the limits of their normal sphere of activities. These beings include clearly mythical ones such as the mountain sprite ["das Wichtelchen"] and personified animals as well as mysterious but recognizably human types such as the swarthy man ["der schwarze Mann"] and Sture Mure, the large maiden. Thus by the first appearance of the novella's thematically central character, the brown girl, the general outlines of overall structure, style, and thematic variation for "Katzensilber" have been narratively formulated. Extended passages of essentially positive characterization and imagery depicting the interaction of ego, initiative, and socialization represented by the "Hof," with its successful relationship to the natural setting, are balanced by depictions of brief but dynamic interactions with agents from beyond that sphere. This general structural and thematic exposition will be modified as the story's narrative momentum moves toward its climax and resolution. The catalyst for this development will be Stifter's brown girl, who is not an unformed childish ego like the boy in "Granit" nor an eccentric but societally attached, and hence ultimately accommodatable persona like the poor priest in "Kalkstein." Instead she proves to be, by virtue of her consistently altruistic personal initiatives, an alien ego which is nonetheless complete in its sense of extrapersonal responsibility and commitment. Stifter appears to posit through this figure not a negation of the universality of the interplay of ego, initiative, and socialization but rather the possibility of limits to its effective application across existential boundaries. There is a tragic aspect in the concept of inadequacy in even the best features of human interaction, such as the authentic love depicted in "Katzensilber;" but there is also, in the final lines of the story, an optimistic intimation that there exists a system of universal evaluation in which the pure and the good are requited wherever they are found. The brown girl is not a flawed heroine whose descent is inevitable—rather she ascends to an individual justification beyond conventional limits.

Once again a detailed textual analysis is needed to fully appreciate the compositional and narrative unity Stifter achieves in formulating this variation of his tripartite thematic interplay. Such features in "Katzensilber" as the seemingly simplistic use of fairy tale-like digressions, repetitive and duplicative contextual and imaginal sequences, and the provocative anonymity of its central figure will be shown to be integral elements of the author's vision for this work.

The first line of "Katzensilber" sets an essentially positive tone for the story's physical setting: "In einem abgelegenen aber sehr schönen Teile unsers Vaterlandes steht ein stattlicher Hof" (221). The region is isolated, but its natural beauty is complemented by the stateliness of the human dwelling which will provide one of the two principal locales for the narrative. The rest of the paragraph continues this balanced descriptive imagery of nature and successful human initiative as represented by the careful husbandry of fruit trees and of other plant life not indigenous to the area. Unlike the ironic significance of the Schauendorf orchards in "Kalkstein," this image of cultivation is rendered nonegocentric by attributing it to the still anonymous owner of the farm. His initiatives seem further objectified by the repeated use of the impersonal "man." The layout of the farmhouse and grounds is also presented in terms of a harmonious distribution of the flowers raised on the estate: some are cultivated in extensive greenhouses, some are tended in the open air, and some of both categories are displayed throughout the rooms of the residence.[1]

The limits of this naturally amalgamated ego, initiative, and socialization format are extended upward in the next two, similarly balanced paragraphs as the descriptive imagery and even word choice continue to highlight the interaction of the farm inhabitants with the natural features of the landscape. In the first paragraph of the pair, the spatial ascent begins at the sandslope behind the greenhouses and proceeds to an evergreen-covered summit. The cliff above the sandslope lends it solidity ["Festigkeit"] by preventing rock slides downward and contributes to the retention of solar heat. The owner has had a solid railing ["festes Geländer"] and benches for rest stops installed on the incline pathway. The imaginal blend of natural and human initiatives is once again conveyed with impersonal "man" and "lassen" constructions continuing the tone of firm amalgamation for the physical setting and hence, by implication, for its inhabitants. The next paragraph expands the descriptive vista outwards so that the concept of "limits" hinted at by the picturesque but closed vista ["beschlossenes Schauspiel"] of the preceding passage can be affirmed as part of an extended pattern of existence characterized by natural boundaries:

> Um das Haus liegen, wie es in jenem Lande immer vorkommt, in nähern und fernern Kreisen Hügel, die mit Feldern und Wiesen bedeckt sind, manches Bauerhaus manchen Meierhof zeigen, und auf dem Gipfel jedes Mal den Wald tragen, der wie nach einem verabredeten Gesetze alle Gipfel jenes hügligen Landes besetzt. (222)

The problematic significance of these boundaries for human interaction is hinted at by the fact that between the hills there are often steep defiles, "ohne das man es ahnt," across whose watercourses there are proper bridges only along the major thoroughfares. Stifter then ends his initial and essential description of the general physical setting for "Katzensilber" with a thematically significant comparison of the northern and southern horizons, from the collective viewpoint of the entire region. To the North, one perceives a steady incline upwards to the dark ["duster"] forests of Bohemia. The alienness of this image contrasts openly with the "friendly blue chain" of the Alps to the South. Sheer height does not appear to be the qualitative factor in this comparison. The northerly slopes are lower but have the potential for harboring unfamiliar forms of existence. Thus, the topographical setting consists of two distinct perceptual dimensions—the successfully amalgamated existential format of the farm and its natural environs versus the potentially problematic physical and psychological limits to that amalgamation, particularly in regard to the northern boundary. Having set the physical scene for the novella, the author now begins to introduce the characters who will provide the narrative interaction.

The hitherto anonymous possessor and engineer of the natural and human amalgamation which the farmstead represents is now given a more detailed identity. His individual initiatives are immediately associated with socializing influences. He has lived in the wider world but as a very young person ["Mensch"] (223). The choice of the word "Mensch" here instead of the word "Mann," especially when juxtaposed with the plural "Menschen" a few words later appears to be one more example of Stifter's capability of constantly building his thematic foundation through an accumulation of connotative elements. When the young man finally did return to his home he pursued an energetic program of refurbishment, the results of which are already outlined in the novella's opening lines. But his individuality, or ego, is systematically diluted in this passage when he is described as a triple heir to much of his present holdings—having inherited them from his father and two bachelor uncles. He also fetches home a city bride from no less than the regional capital to share his farmstead. The fact that they marry in the small parish church in his lonely province ["trauliche Einöde"] is quickly balanced by the fact that they regularly revisit the capital as well:

Wenn es aber Winter wurde, dann ging er mit der Gattin in ihre Geburtsstadt, um eine Weile dort zu sein, und zu sehen, was die Menschen indessen wieder gefördert, was auf geistigem Felde sich zugetragen und im Zusammenleben sich geändert hat. (223)

The arrangement of the tripartite object of the verb "sehen" in the last clause of this passage identifies the urban connection as an important element or perhaps even the cultural base of the amalgam of ego, initiative, and socialization represented by the farm. Priority is given firstly to the ideal of human advancement, secondly to the intellectual basis for it, and thirdly and summatively to its application to the realities of communal existence. The passage as a whole then not only establishes the socialized character of two of the story's main figures, but it also completes the first cycle of a topographically vertical narrative progression which continues to alternate throughout the novella. This verticality is central to developing the thematic variation dealing with the limits of a particular existential model and with the problems of cross-over socialization growing out of that model. The cyclical segment and passage end together with an image reestablishing the natural positivity of the farmstead. It is formally posited as the physical center for the thematic interplay of ego, initiative, and socialization in "Katzensilber" with the brief but somehow resolute statement, "Mit der Rückkehr der Sonne kam er wieder auf seinen Hof" (223).

The next paragraph introduces another major character of the story, the landowner's mother. This venerable matron is described as one who has hardly ever traveled beyond her native province and its environs, having only visited the capital once in her long life. She is loving towards her city-bred "daughter," but she forms a charming contrast in her rustic apparel as she goes about with her modish younger relation. (Clothing as representative of specific social orientations will be seen to assume increasing significance as the story continues.[2]) Because the mother has almost never traveled and because she is so totally integrated with the life of the farm, it is fittingly she who will interact at the upper limits of the "Hof" when the unknown girl first appears. During the winter while her son is maintaining the cultural amalgamation of the farm with its urban base below, the mother maintains the vertical center of the narrative by tending the farm during his winter sojourns in the city. She descends only in spirit as she watches the servant go to fetch her children in the spring, "wenn der Wagen den Hügel hinab fuhr" (224). The vertical aspects of the narrative setting are again sensed when the succeeding short paragraph reiterates the social nature of the son's efforts upon returning, as he directs his workers in refurbishing the farm and tending to the work in the fields. The structural and stylistic features of even this brief passage seem crafted to maintain the tonal underpinning of the thematic interplay. The master of the farm is active ["tätig"], but his egoism and initiative are diffused by the appellation "Sohn," the use of the passive, the impersonal "man" as subject, and the contrastive connotation of the possessive "sein" with the collectives "Gesinde" and "Leute." Already at this early point in the novella there is a positive cast to the amalgam of ego, initiative, and socialization represented by the farm with its union of rural, natural, and urban elements. This positive picture will not change; ironically, however, it will provide one side of the ultimately tragic encounter between "good" representatives from incompatible worlds. That encounter in turn will express the essence of Stifter's thematic variation in "Katzensilber."

There now begins in the text a series of shorter paragraphs which develop an additional aspect of the Hof amalgam, equally important for the later exposition of the thematic variation. Under a divine aegis, the family nucleus at the farm begins to expand: "Nach zwei Jahren schickte der Himmel einen Zuwachs der Familie, es erschien das Töchterlein Emma" (224). The hierarchical aspect of organized socialization is expressed in the shift of the adult character designations from "Sohn," "Tochter," and "Mutter" to "Vater," "Mutter," and "Großmutter" respectively. The integrative nature of this development is emphasized by the charming image of the grandmother's tutelage of the new mother in matters maternal. The process of family growth ["Zuwachsen"] continues with the birth of the dark-haired little sister, Clementia. It is significant that in introducing this second child Stifter contrasts her hair color with with that of her older sibling. The concept of individual differences is being introduced, which at this point seems to affirm the naturally evolved socialization available to childish egos ensconced within an established tradition of familial behavioral patterns. The new members of the extended farm family are also quickly integrated into the cyclical, vertical narrative structure of the story by being included in the winter journey down to the city and back up again to the farm. The supremacy of the social amalgam appears to be balanced with the assurance of individual accommodation when the returned travelers retire to their "Gelasse" (a connotatively diminishing term roughly equivalent to "bedchambers"), which have been rendered even more comfortable ["noch wohnlicher"] through the initiative of the most completely integrated farm inhabitant, the grandmother. This balance of individualizing and integrative imagery continues for two additional short paragraphs; the girls are jointly described as growing taller and having similarly charming facial features, but "das eine hatte . . . die blonden seidenweichen Locken des Vaters, das andere die schwarzen der Mutter." A prioritization of values is also expressed here indirectly, in that the parents despite their opposite complexions are already established co-participants in the amalgam that is the farm. There is, too, reiteration of the imagery of nature and of ascent which is so important for developing the thematic variation in "Katzensilber." The growth of the children is termed "growing up" ["emporwachsen"]; and their gentle socialization by the grandmother, although it begins in her room, progresses steadily away from the residence to the garden, to the arbor, and finally to the already designated limits of the farmstead proper, the greenhouses and sandslope. This thematically significant imaginal movement outward and upward takes on a more narrational form when the children, whose youthful bodies continue to strive upward ["emporzielen"], are described as being fit to accompany the old lady to the high Nußberg (225). The intimation that this nutting expedition is something approaching the upper limits of the established amalgam of socialized human initiative and natural phenomena is present in the fact that it transpires after the principal farming activities are completed. It is also expressed through a, for this novella, relatively rare use of inanimate personifications: "Wenn der Haber bleichte, und das Korn und die Gerste in der Scheune zur Ruhe war, dann färbten sich die Haselnüsse mit braunen oder rosenfarbenen Wänglein" (225). The next several paragraphs seem to indicate by their length and textual density that Stifter intends a significant expansion of his setting, characterization, and vertically arranged narrative progression in order to establish their optimal limits prior to the appearance of his thematically central figure, "das braune Mädchen."

As they venture away from the farmhouse, the farm children are adequately equipped representatives of their naturally amalgamated world, bent on a productive exploitation of its fruits. Their shoes are constructed to protect their feet from the sharp gravel as they climb, and they are outfitted with baskets and harvesting implements in the form of rods with hooks at the ends for lowering the limbs of the hazel bushes. Limits for their initiatives seem to be carefully kept in the foreground however: the nutting rods themselves are made from hazel branches, and images of natural power such as the cliffs are combined with others such as "Händchen," "Geländer," "rasten," and "Bänklein" which point up human limitations (225). This innocuous introduction of the concept of limits seems to foreshadow the major implications they will have later for the viability of the farmstead amalgam at its upper physical boundaries. These boundaries will, in turn, be pivotal to the central thematic variation in "Katzensilber": the problem of transenvironmental socialization. But for the time being, the concept of limits is suspended within the general description of energetic but still integrated activities of the nutting party. A second aspect of this same passage, which will make its own important contribution to the continuing development of the novella's thematic variation, is the universal propensity of children to respond to the sensuous appeal of phenomena which may have no commensurate practical worth. The young sisters diligently pry shining flakes of mica from rocks they find lying about their resting places and carefully collect them for later transport home as valued and attractive momentos. This initiative on behalf of a naively intuited worth can be seen as a metaphorical prefiguration of the children's later affinity for their exotic playmate and of the common appreciation of nature's "treasures" which cements that friendship. The verbal triplet here which outlines the grandmother's reactions reflects her more practical outlook: "Die Großmutter wartete auf sie, oder half ihnen, oder erzählte Geschichten" (225). The passage then concludes with a suspensive mixture of images which suggest the separateness of the higher environs of the homestead, with others that suggest the assimilability of the entire surrounding vista within the perceptual mosaic of the farm children. The idea of the upper landscape as a separate existential sphere is suggested in the assertion that: "Wenn sie noch höher hinauf kamen, da war wieder die Erde . . ." This concept is also supported by the series of individual natural phenomena which then follows—"Haidekraut," "Gräser," "Kräuter," "Wacholderstrauch," "Birkenstrunk," and "Distel." Amidst these enumerated features of an implicitly sovereign realm, the human initiative is temporarily halted as the nutting party stops to rest. (Again it is interesting to note here the vertical connotation of "sit down" ["niedersetzen"] for this limiting action.) The topographical isolation of the group's position is also reflected in the view of cultivated fields and human habitations below and by the fact that the viewers themselves are the only "white points" on the mountain. But coming full circle the distant peaks are then characterized by their weak cliffs ["schwachen Felsen"] and little tablets ["Täfelchen"] of snow (226). This latter image seems formally reminiscent of the children's coveted mica flakes mentioned above. The generally suspensive tone of this mixture of perceptual viewpoints with imaginal contrasts points to the coming thematic conflict. That conflict arises from the recognition that even a positively established format for the universal human interplay of ego, initiative, and socialization such as that represented by the farm must by dint of material reality have its effective limits.

Stifter, as great a literary artist as he shows himself to be in this story and in his other *Bunte Steine*, may have felt some editorial pressure to consider his predominantly bourgeois reading public in the portrayal of a humanly sympathetic and charming but also materially successful social amalgam, such as that represented by the farm. If indeed such a pressure existed, it would be skillfully addressed in the two contextually and thematically significant passages which come next (226-27). The Grandmother tells her resting charges, in a suitably elevated setting where "die hohen Halmen wankten," the tale of Sture Mure, the large maiden. The story is from recent local lore and tells how a mysterious brown-skinned girl comes to work for the "Hagenbucher," a farmer whose homestead is located "wo dort hinter dem spitzigen Walde die weißen Wolken ziehen . . ." The imagery of height, together with the connotations of hardy coarseness and insularity present in the name *Hagenbucher* (cf. *Hag*: enclosure, *hagebuch*: hornbeam birch, and *hagebuchen*: coarse), precedes the description of this harsh ["streng"] man whose requirements no single servant can satisfy. Sture Mure, however, is equal to the task and asks only for food and "manchmal ein Tuch auf einen Rock und ein Linnen auf ein Hemd." This capable person comes from an alien realm, as evidenced by her brunette visage (which contrasts the whiteness of the "hornbeam birch") and her prodigious physical abilities. Her only need beyond her bodily requisites is for clothing, an implicit symbol of social integration. This particular instance of the clothing motif in "Katzensilber" appears to represent a continuation of its thematic significance for the entire work. The clothing motif is, however, only one of the ways in which the Sture Mure episode condenses the already discussed allusions to a limited format for the ego, initiative, and socialization interplay into a concise preview of the narrational and thematic whole of "Katzensilber." Stifter again chooses to use subjunctives in a context where they are grammatically acceptable, but where they also seem to impart a quality of dubiety to the narration. The attempt of Sture Mure to cross over into conventional society is doomed to fail as will be that of her alter-ego in the outer narrative, "das braune Mädchen." The former character, like the latter, also demonstrates a willingness to contribute to the existential format into which she enters, and she shows great facility in mastering and even improving upon its patterns of productive initiative. She remains at the Hagenbuch house as a permanent resident for years. But when the "Hagenbucher" repeats a strange message he has heard coming from the shadows of the forest as he returns home from market, the effect is astonishing. Upon hearing the words, "sag der Sture Mure, die Rauh-Rinde sei tot," the large maiden runs sobbing from the house never to be heard from again (226). The mysterious source of the message and its totally disruptive effect on the maiden's ostensible "trans-socialization" point forcefully to the reemergence in her own heart and mind of memories of her native existence. Her sobs express her tragic awareness of the ultimate futility of her endeavor and the ego-affective loss she has sustained. It is important for the later exposition of the work's thematic variation of "limits" to note here that there is no implicit censure or negativity attributable either to the recognizable, if only marginal socialization format of the Hagenbuch farm or to the unknown origins of Sture Mure. For Stifter and his audience the salient features of the two adult figures described above were no doubt the positive ones of initiative and hard work. Hence, the commitment of the one character to his own hard-won existential format, as evidenced by the sweating anxiety with which he flees the alien voice in the wood, clashes with the sudden and violently realized recommitment of the other character to her alien world. The natural harshness of the setting's upper topographical limits echoed in the connotations of the person and place names "Hagenbucher," " Sture Mure," "Gallbrunerwald," "Jochträger," and "Rauh-Rinde" has conditioned socialization patterns for individuals, limiting their scope of personal initiatives for long-range fulfillment and integration within a cultural base. The tragic dilemma of Sture Mure and ultimately of the brown girl also is that the more successful they are in assimilating positive forms of ego, initiative, and socialization in their own world, the more apt they become to attempt a similarly productive interaction with another, attractive but essentially different cultural sphere. And it seems the more they are accepted into that other world, the longer they are kept from finishing their own native developmental pattern.

Any doubts that this idea of limited formats for socialization and the potentially tragic consequences of crossing those limits will both be of central thematic importance in "Katzensilber" should be dispelled by the almost immediate juxtaposition of a second narrative digression, the tale of the mountain sprite ["das Wichtelchen"] (227). It is interesting that Stifter puts this second parabolic prefiguration of his thematic variation in an explicitly supernatural, fairy tale context. But the narrative thrust of this brief but vividly expressive anecdote is exactly the same as that in the Sture Mure episode: a being of alien existential form comes into the upper topographical plane of a conventional social setting (represented by the Karesberg settlement), renders capable and valuable service, but ultimately fails to maintain its new social connection and disappears. The sprite asks only for a piece of white bread in return for his careful and productive tending of the village sheep. This type of bread no doubt represents a degree of refinement and sophistication possible in a more civilized environment than the creature is used to, but it is still within the bounds of acceptable transcultural negotiation. The villagers, however, alter the bargain in an attempt to reward the creature's faithful service and one evening leave it a pretty red jacket as well. The tiny goatherd dons its new garment and leaps further and further down the mountain as if wild with joy (227). It might be argued that the sprite has perhaps now completed the first step of integration with its new world and has descended towards an even more complete assimilation with the larger population centers of the lowlands. But it must be remembered that one of the primary conditions of the bargain was that besides the bread, the villagers were not allowed to ["dürften nicht"] give him any reward. The connotations of prohibition and dubiety provided by the choice of "dürfen" in its subjunctive form together with the other subjunctives in the opening lines of the passage suggest a questionable situation. (This connotative use of the subjunctive was also much in evidence in the immediately preceding Sture Mure tale.) The red-clad sprite is also described as hopping across green meadows like a fire—an image of self-consumptive, irrational initiative set against a passively constant background. The expression "gar nie wieder" then underscores the fact that he never ever appears again. Typically, Stifter seems to back away from or suspend any too-definitive statement of his thematic viewpoint here, once he has sketched out its broad outlines and has set the general ideational direction of his narrative.

There is an additional compositional stroke involved in the juxtaposition of these two very similar digressions. Sture Mure, a being with a normal human form, apparently failed in her attempt to cross over into conventional society mainly because of a need to fulfill some undefined obligation in her native existential sphere. Her sole agency for trans-socialization was "der Hagenbucher," himself a marginal representative of the conventional world, whose interaction with the maiden seemed to follow her own dictates. The sprite, a clearly unreal phenomenon, fails in its crossover attempt in the process of direct negotiation with a collective social body representing the human world. Stifter gives in the tale of Sture Mure a preview of his theme and then restates it immediately using a figure who is patently unreal. The author must be relying on an associative process in the reader's mind to consolidate this dual prefiguration: the alien figures are thematically interchangeable in the two tales and this prepares the reader for the advent of the central figure in the main narrative, the brown girl. Her nature like that of Sture Mure is human and socialized, but like the sprite she will embody the consequential limitations of interaction between separately evolved existential formats.

The eventual appearance of the brown girl will be part of a narrational cycle similar to the ones developed in the Sture Mure and sprite episodes cited above. The new cycle will include a similarly positive portrayal of an amalgam of nature and society, represented this time by the family, servants, and activities of the farmstead. And they too will operate within the spatially vertical context of the novella's topographical settings. The paragraph which immediately follows the tale of the sprite, and returns the reader to the outer narrative, mixes detailed descriptions of sensory perceptions shared by the nutting party with individualized, even personified descriptions of the flora and fauna of the upper landscape (227). The children and their keeper proceed through the wild plum and alder bushes where they see beetles, flies, and butterflies and hear the sounds of buntings, hedgesparrows, and wrens. They observe a circling chicken hawk and the smooth brown rind of the birch trees beneath the shedding silver bark. They move on to the oaks with their strong, knotty limbs and dark, stiff leaves; and they finally reach the evergreen stand where the pines sough ["sausen"], the spruce stand about with their green hair hanging down ["mit herabhängenden grünen Haaren"], and the firs spread out their gleaming needles. Looking back from the vantage point of this sovereign, variegated natural "community," the party perceives their home and garden below as tiny, and the panes of the distant greenhouses sparkle like the little flakes of mica they have broken out of the stone (227). This last image, likening the domestic base of operation to a natural curiosity, ironically reinforces the concept of separate but equally integral worlds and the vertical format of the border zone between them is developed further. The thematically supportive cycle of imagery and action continues, as the next paragraph balances another series of natural individuations with instances of human initiative. It is interesting also that the description of human activities balances limitations against initiatives:

the party is unable to gather various types of berries because of the season, but the father's prodigious improvements of the trail are recognized as is the anonymous activity of the summer wood-cutting. Lest human activity be shown in perhaps too strong a light, Stifter also combines his images of initiative with the deenergizing "lassen" and "werden" of impersonal and passive constructions (228). After the delicate combining of natural entities and human initiatives to reiterate the tone of peaceful amalgamation represented by the world of the farmstead, or "Hof," there is a brief but pointed allusion to its upper limit, the high Nußberg. This landmark is additionally elevated in that it rises up from yet another topographical descent: " Sie sahen nun einen grauen Rasen vor sich . . ., dann war ein Tal, und dann stand der hohe Nußberg empor" (228). There then comes another short, reiterative paragraph which echoes the vertical narrative traverse of "abwärts" and "empor." This echo is joined with a presentation of lively but diminutive natural phenomenon and with energetic human initiatives. The description of the latter, however, seems again mitigated by the use of the causative "lassen." The imaginal fusion finally ends as the group arrives at the threshold of the upper-most area of the narrational environs:

> Da gingen sie nun auf dem Rasen abwärts, . . . in dem ein Wässerlein floß. Sie gingen zwischen den grauen Steinen, auf denen . . . die Bachstelze hüpfte und mit den Steuerfedern den Takt schlug. Und als sie zu dem Bächlein gekommen waren, in welchem die grauen, flinken Fischlein schwimmen, und um welches die blauen, schönen Wasserjungfern flattern, und als sie über den breiten Stein gegangen waren, den ihnen der Vater als Brücke über das Bächlein hatte legen lassen, kamen sie gegen den hohen Nußberg empor. (228)

The nut mountain represents the uppermost limits, both topographically and thematically for the interactive form of ego, initiative, and socialization represented by the farmstead and its natural environs. It will become evident as the story progresses, however, that the mountain is nonetheless an integral part of that amalgam. This symbolic import of the setting is further established in the next series of paragraphs which go on to depict the various activities and perceptions of the children and their grandmother once they have ascended the mountain (229). There is a continued contrastive but balanced mingling of images from nature and society. The summit of the mountain is put into greater relief by the rocks lying at its feet, and the variety of the shrubbery at the top forms a counterpoint to the vista of tilled fields and distant regions below. The fact that it is strangers ["fremde Menschen"] who are working these fields, and that the regions are unknown ["unbekannt"] combines the idea of upper limits with a concept of separate though conventionally similar forms of social existence. The second paragraph of the passage focuses again momentarily on the integration of egocentristic and collective actions by the farm community. The grandmother leads the darkhaired child by the hand, but the blonde goes alone jumping ably over the rocks (229). The three characters are again separately named but form a charming collective endeavor as they stoop down, one by one, to enter the hazelbush enclosure. At this point their efforts are joined with those of the natural denizens of the area whose activities are likewise a mixture of individual and collective efforts: "Da waren nun sie und viele andere Dinge auf dem Berge." The tiny red mice are busy as a group gathering food and nesting materials for their young while the solitary jay and stealthy squirrel each pursue their individual sustenance. The designation of this varied activity on the nut mountain as the quest for individualized joy and pleasure ["Freude und Lust"] duplicates in a more natural setting the model for accommodation of the individual within the group, as represented by the human society of the farm described earlier (See above p. 119).

In the second of three paragraphs of similar length and imaginal density which constitute the core of this passage, the focus shifts to the actual nutting activities of the party. These initiatives highlight once again the positive exploitation of the topographical amalgam by its human participants. The children bend the nut-laden branches (which in their natural state point up towards the blue heavens) downward and harvest the ripening hazel nuts. If their individual efforts are not successful, their grandmother's assistance teaches them the benefit of group effort. The old lady limits herself to bending the limbs while the girls do the actual plucking. The paragraph ends with additional activity which is nowise associated with the productive exploitation of nature.

The sisters wander about the area after their nutting task is completed. A series of diminutives in this passage ("Körbchen," "Täschlein," "Tüchlein") serves to deemphasize the impact of human activity. The girls then climb to the summit where they sit down on an ancient, very inviting hazel root and while away the time "in the broad sparkling air" ["in der weiten, glänzenden Luft"].

The openness of this last image, which also suggests a pure, childlike impulse to survey existential boundaries, seems to set the scene for the thematically supportive digressions which follow it. The third, structurally similar paragraph of the passage brings the duplicative narrational cycle full circle when the grandmother begins again with stories to entertain the resting children. The atmosphere is right for reevoking the lateral thematic possibilities at the upper limits, where separate but positive modes of existence can apparently coexist and even merge. But it is the separateness of the different elevations which is emphasized this time, as the tales are limited to only the schematic mention—expressed in the subjunctive—of the exertions of a pair of legendary fowl which suffered physical privation in their encounter with the heights. The realm of real human activity below is reduced to a tiny scale: "weiße(n) Pünktlein, die kaum zu sehen waren und ein Haus oder eine Ortschaft bedeuteten" (230). The natural features of the landscape are reviewed in more detail, but the mixture of positive, negative, and ambiguous descriptors produces a tonal ambivalence in regard to the upper elevations. There are the marvelous names of the mountains ["wunderlichen Namen der Berge"] and the very pure, beautiful distance of the heavens ["gar reine, schöne Himmelsferne"], but the peaks are strange ["seltsam"] and must be deciphered ["enträtselt"]; the clouds can be weak ["schwach"] and suggestive of unknown things. The most significant descriptive detail here contains a pointed association with the Sture Mure and sprite episodes from the immediately previous narrative cycle. This allusion occurs through the reappearance of the local names of the Gallbrunerwald and the Karesberge, which are here associated with the connotatively equivocal directional term "towards midnight" ("gegen Mitternacht") and a cloud of diminished beauty ("eine lange, matte Wolke . . ., die nicht so schön glänzte wie die gegen Mittag, über dem Gebirge").

This reevocation of a potentially negative dimension for the upper region of the farm amalgam is followed by three shorter paragraphs which restate contrastively positive aspects of its middle and lower strata (231). The grandmother's narrative sketches are again only outlined in a schematic fashion, but in contrast to the single, mythical anecdote of the little rooster cited above they now involve a list of human types and activities, all expressed in the indicative. Galloping knights and pavilioned ladies from the historical past provide a transition to examples of alpine existence more closely related to the farm—shepherds, anglers, and hunters. In any case, the nutting party physically responds to this downward shift of context by embarking on their own way down the mountain. The reestablishment of the farm as both the physical center of the vertically perceived topological setting of the story and the social center for its present character constellations is prepared for in the second and third paragraphs of the passage: "Sie ordneten die zerdrückten Kleidchen, nahmen Korb und Rute, und gingen auf dem nämlichen Wege hinab, auf dem sie gekommen waren" (231). Hence, the socialization symbol of proper clothing seems to be combined with the already mentioned balance of amalgamation images which Stifter developed for the ascent. The phenomena of higher up—the bushes, stones, brook, fish, dragonflies, meadow, woods, and crag—blend naturally into the sandslope, greenhouses and lower meadow of the central farmstead. Even the lowermost symbolic limits of the farm amalgam are represented by the figure of the city-bred mother coming to greet them in her beautiful clothing and with her parasol.

The cyclical segment of the novella which introduced the sisters, followed their integration into the social and natural setting of the farm, and then transported them to the upper limits of that amalgamation ends as it began. The final paragraph of this particular segment of the vertically formulated narration depicts again the loving socialization process provided for the youthful egos by their own supervised activities and those of their mentor, the grandmother. The busy enterprise of the nut gathering is now extended to the arena of home and hearth. The droll features of the children's nutcrackers introduce an element of play into the nutting initiative, and the grandmother uses the nuts as gifts which further consolidate the family:

> In die Mäuler der Nussknacker taten sie die Nüsse, ... und zerbrachen sie, indem die Knacker ... erschreckliche Gesichter erzeugten. Sie gaben von den Kernen und den Nüssen dem Vater und der Mutter und auch der Großmutter, die selten Nüsse von dem hohen Nußberge mitbrachte, und dann immer nur wenige, die sie stets auf das Tischlein der Kinder legte, sowie sie auch die geschenkten ihnen immer wieder zurückschenkte. (231)

Stifter begins his next reiterative segment of the narrative cycle with another addition to the farm society—the new baby brother, Sigismund. The birth is immediately set in relation to the continuing cultural integration of the sisters. The girls are again individualized as "Blondköpfchen" and "Schwarzköpfchen" but are united in the collective endeavor of learning their educational basics from a tutor brought from the city. The physical attributes of the little boy provide a physical correlate of this social assimilation, as he combines in his brown curls and brown eyes the contrasting features of his blond, blue-eyed father and his sister Emma and those of his brunette, black-eyed mother and his sister Clementia. The significance that this unifying figure will have for the thematic variation of separate formats of social existence is foreshadowed by the irony that all contact with the elevated locale where their limits will converge must be temporarily suspended as the boy undergoes the necessary integration with the middle and lower strata of the farm amalgam (232). Sigismund, or "Braunköpfchen," proceeds spatially as his siblings did from the house to the garden, to the orchards, and finally to the outlying limits of the farm proper, the greenhouses. He participates in two winter sojourns in the capital below and undergoes a period of physical adaption as he follows his sisters about the fields and woods of the farmstead.

The author condenses these events into two very short paragraphs and quickly returns his positively integrated characters to the upper topographical limits of their social existence, the nut mountain, where they will soon experience a contact from beyond those limits.

The cycle continues structurally and contextually with another ascent by the farm children and their grandmother to the hazelnut bushes. The consistent adjectival designation of "high" ["hoch"] in regard to the upper locale maintains a blend of realistic and symbolic values. The children are again individualized by hair coloration and physical competencies, yet the girls' similar clothing and implements and their repeated returns to their slower younger brother re-evoke the concept of ego integration for the individual within the group initiative. The narrative focus of the passage is on the encouragement given the boy to participate. The gradualness and continuity of this process contrasts with the abruptness of the cross-over socialization from one existential sphere to another depicted in the Sture Mure episode. Reiterating this developmental sequence also seems to underscore the positive nature of the farm complex in anticipation of the nonjudgmental but tragic resolution of the story's later crisis. Also in preparation for the thematically central plot complication of their encounter with the brown girl, the nutting party again concludes its exploitation of the natural resources by sitting upon the thick old hazelroot and enjoying another tale from the grandmother's repertoire (233).

This time the tale centers upon the remarkable consequences an alien encounter has for another marginal representative of the here-and-now existential sphere. The story of the bloody light ["das blutige Licht"] is told in a single paragraph, as were the other anecdotes. But the greater length, the more frequent use of the subjunctive, and the darkly ambiguous imagery all indicate an increase in complexity. A simple shepherd is approached by a swarthy man as he tends his flock. The man gives him a cryptic message that: "in der Harthöhle, wo das Silber rinne, das Blutige Licht sei" (233). In contrast to Sture Mure and the sprite, the shepherd is not a self-motivated character who embarks upon an ill-fated, ego-generated initiative to integrate with an alien form of existence. He is rather, a successful agent within his own existential format, and he takes no action other than to wait for further word from his swarthy visitor. The stranger, however, never appears again, and it is only in the course of the shepherd's normal initiatives that the situation finds a resolution. In search of a lost lamb, which he hears bleating again and again higher up, the shepherd arrives at an elevation which is apparently above his normal range (and hence a symbol for a form of existence beyond the norm). He perceives the connection between the "silver" of the swarthy man's message and the gleaming torrent which he finds issuing from a cave high up in the streambed. After much exertion the shepherd reaches the cave and penetrates deeper into this alien realm, where he finds a glowing red stone glimmering from no apparent light source. This last detail accentuates the uncanniness of the situation, although the shepherd's ascent beyond his normal limits appears not to have jeopardized his established social function. This is evidenced by the fact that his lost lamb has returned on its own and is nursing at the udder of its ewe. The stone, which possesses the eerie power of self-illumination and influence over other entities, as expressed in the shepherd's stark impulse to possess it, continues to evince ego-affective properties. It shines within its covering of common fieldstone and throws sparks on things when handled. The ambiguous properties of this gem, expressed in the subjunctive, lead the shepherd to carefully wrap and preserve his exotic find. This action stands in contrast to the children's innocent gathering of mica flakes in the outer narrative, and the danger and greed inherent in it seem somehow out of place in the mountain world. The shepherd barters the stone with an alpine farmer for five sheep, a positive acquisition in the context of his own naturally amalgamated existence. The continuing resale of the stone brings to light a new aspect in the positive portrayal of the agrarian way of life. The professions, provenances, and profits of the successive possessors of the gem seem to demonstrate a clear topographical and implicitly evaluative "descent" from the mysterious austerity of its alpine origin. The farmer trades it to a doctor for a horse, an acceptable and necessary adjunct to rural life, but an intrinsically more egoistic possession than five sheep. The doctor, always one of the more socialized and city-connected rural types, sells the stone to a Lombard for one hundred gold pieces. Thus the enterprise moves into the realm of purely commercial interaction. The Lombard, representing a geographically distant existential sphere, has the stone refined and cut, from whence its pieces reach the courts of kings and princes, the pinnacle of social organization. It is doubtful that Stifter intended to suggest any inherent bipolarity in persons or things from the upper elevations. The mysterious messenger is a potentially sinister, dark figure, but so, too, was the harmless messenger for the totally sympathetic Sture Mure. And there was actually a warning in the dark man's metaphorical designation of the jewel as "das blutige Licht." It is, in fact, the institutions which are outside the cultural and vocational parameters of mountain life, the foreign sovereignties, which bring out the "blood" in the stone: ". . . sie beneiden sich darum, und wenn sie das Land erobern, wird der Stein sorgsam fortgetragen, als ob man eine eroberte Stadt in einem Schächtelchen davon trüge (233). One notes here the final subjunctive "punctuation" applied to this questionable sphere of social existence. Neither aspect of the novella's rural setting, the conventional nor the exotic, must be made too ambivalent—only their interaction with each other.

Stifter appears to envision the farmstead as a union of nature and society which is not only topographically limited at its upper boundaries, but which is also relatively secure from outside initiatives generated by the collective egoism of the world below. The ordering of the grandmother's stories in pairs continues when she goes on to tell of prospectors from an earlier era: "seltsame Menschen, die weit von der Ferne gekommen sind, das Gold in unsern Bächen gewaschen und sind reich von dannen gezogen . . ." (234). The orientation of these two anecdotes shifts from the patently mythical to the more practically plausible, as in the sprite and Sture Mure tales respectively. But as in that earlier thematic duality, the solid nature of the indigenous society is the core of this pairing as well. The locals successfully and temporarily imitate the prospecting activities of the outlanders, but they then return to the traditional use of the streams to water livestock. The grandmother ends by indicating the limited application of any further mineral exploitation of the region: mussel pearls from the local waters adorn pretty women and holy icons. There may be an implied connection in this last image with the figure of the mother, the lovely representative of the farm society's broader cultural base. The mention of icons in this context seems also to imply that the preparation of such ornaments is a sanctified occupation.

The two-part anecdotal digression analyzed above supports the development of theme but not the progress of the narrative. Its effect is purposely not diminished by the one-sentence paragraph which follows it, expressing as it does the descent of the grandmother and the children and completing this cycle of the vertically oriented narrative. The author states simply: "Wenn die Kinder und die Großmutter lange gesessen waren, standen sie wieder auf und gingen nach Hause" (235). The past perfect and preterite tenses here, in addition to expressing a chronological sequence, also seem to convey an order of priority with the reflective period at the upper limits being preeminent over the actions of rising and going. The next paragraph, however, clearly shifts the field of imagery to environs lower down, even if not all the way to the farm itself. The assertive "Aber" at the paragraph's beginning effectively brings the reader's attention to bear on the other nature outings of the farm children. They visit the surrounding meadows, wild strawberry hills, and fields, enjoying a variety of floral color and beauty. But along with this imagery of a harmonious natural milieu are details which seem to maintain spatial and characterizational links with the earlier passage depicting the rural reaction to outside intrusions. The forget-me-not flowers with their clear "Fischäuglein" ["little fish eyes"] are reminiscent of the higher-lying minnow pool; and they end as a gift to the mother, which ties them associatively with the mussel pearls given to beautiful ladies. The children prefer the smaller but sweeter wild strawberries to the domestic ones grown by their father on his lower-lying sand slope. Hence, it is becoming apparent that the children, although lovingly integrated within the social format of the farmstead and increasingly capable of applying their individual initiatives to the collective exploitation of its natural environs, still possess enough innocent egoism to respond openly to phenomena from the upper limits of their own world. Stifter appears to have carefully developed this characterization in preparation for the children's encounter and interaction with the brown girl. As securely established members of the ego, initiative, and socialization interplay represented by the farm-nature amalgam, who nonetheless still have an instinctive appreciation of the novel and exotic, they are the logical candidates for accepting this representative from another realm. This thematically supportive characterization is consolidated in the last paragraph before the appearance of "das braune Mädchen."

The farm children, although failing in their attempt to imitate the prospecting activities of their historical countrymen, are no doubt content with the sensory beauties they experience in the process (remembering their earlier fascination with the mica flakes). The general pleasantness of tone and imagery is unmistakable here:

> Für sich allein standen die Kinder gerne am Bache, wo es sanft fließt und allerlei krause Linie zieht, und blickten auf den Sand, der wohl wie Gold war, wenn die Sonne durch das Wasser auf ihn schien, und der glänzende Blättchen und Körner zeigte. Wenn sie aber mit einem Schaufelchen Sand herausholten und gut wuschen und schwemmten, so waren die Blättchen Katzensilber, und die Körner waren schneeweiße Stückchen von Kiesel. (235)

The single mention of the mineral substance from the novella's title occurs in this passage, which clearly marks it as an important thematic orientation point as well as a narrational point of departure. It is also important to note at this juncture in the work, a scant one sentence away from the first appearance of the story's pivotal figure, "das braune Mädchen," that the vertical narrative orientation has remained suspended at the upper limits of the Nußberg. The more thematically central role which this verticality plays, in comparison to the similar up-and-down structure cited for "Kalkstein" with its ascent and descent between the parsonage and the limestone hills, is a consequence of the thematic variation in "Katzensilber": existential boundaries and hence boundaries of socialization. The focus on the upper limits of the work's central setting seems narrationally logical, then, for the introduction of the child from another world. And Stifter, after a detailed introduction of this central figure, will accelerate his narrated "ups and downs" in a series of short, dynamically phrased scenes which establish the kinetic nature of almost all of the girl's subsequent appearances in the novella. The resulting contrast with the more static depictions and characterizations of the farm inhabitants will be compositional parallel to the thematic question of equally positive, but culturally nonsynchronous forms of socialization.

The implicit positivity on the "other side" of the existential limits, i.e., for the extra-narrative provenance of "das braune Mädchen," although often overlooked by critics, is clearly manifest in the first description given of her. The farm children are depicted as even more fit than during previous outings for this unique encounter, having grown still more beautiful and wondrous ["schöner und wunderbarer"]; and the brown girl's initial attribute "fremd" ["strange"] is quickly balanced by the statement that she is almost as tall and yet slimmer than "Blondköpfchen" (236). So as an individual, the brown girl is implicitly a physical equal of the other attractive children. But the thematically pregnant designation of "fremd," given first, is re-evoked by the third descriptive detail regarding the girl—her naked arms. It can be noted as the story progresses, that there is mention of particular limbs and body parts (excluding hair and eye color) only in relation to the alien girl. This contrast of bare arms with the clothing of the farm inhabitants is another motif used to further the novella's thematic evolution. And there is also the connection of these arms with the limbs of the capable but ultimately tragic Sture Mure remarked upon earlier (226). As to the brown girl's own clothing, her sleeveless and collarless jersey and her "grüne Höschen," while not intrinsically ambivalent features, do quickly consolidate the impression of differentness which will remain with this figure throughout the remainder of the story. The many red ribbons of her otherwise simple attire may be an attempt by the girl to emulate similar adornments on the dresses and hats of the farm children mentioned earlier (223). The great quantity of them, however, in contrast to the unspecified amount on the girls' dresses seems to be another indication of a perhaps too-energetic willingness to "cross-over," as was again the case with Sture Mure. The final detail of the black eyes, which are reminiscent of the mother figure, who represents the opposite end of the existential verticality, adds one more touch of ambivalence to this ostensibly alien creature. It should also be noted that this entire encounter takes place at the ancient hazel root where the thematic outlines of the story have already been expressed in symbolic tales. Thus, Stifter's ability to encapsulate his overall thematic statement in a compact series of images and character relationships, as in the opening passages of "Granit," appears once again evident here. There also is the inclusion by a single descriptive stroke of the thematically supportive, vertically traversed physical background. The balance begun here between positive and ambivalent images surrounding the brown girl will become the chief narrational means of creating the thematic tension and suspense which will only be resolved, and then tragically, in the final lines of "Katzensilber."

A sense of gradualness seems to combine with an accelerating structural pattern in the several shorter paragraphs which follow the brown girl's debut. These lines include her shy departure from the first meeting and a schematic reference to the descent of the farm party. But there are also several thematically relevant details in the description of their second encounter. The girl again appears, not while the group pursues its integrated activity of nutting, but during the reflective hazel root interlude; and she reacts to being addressed by withdrawing partially into the bushes, which, significantly, hide her naked arms, the symbol of her differentness. When she flees this time, it is downward ["hinunter"], suggesting that the realm from which she comes also has its verticality and must in some way parallel the topography of the farm world. When the children begin to request more frequent visits to the high Nußberg to see the brown girl, the grandmother obliges them; but paradoxically the strange girl is often not to be seen. It is important to remark this additional allusion to a separate extra-narrative sphere of existence for the brown girl. Such references become increasingly rare and understated as the narrative focuses more and more on her transcultural interaction. But if the thematic variation in "Katzensilber" is to revolve around the inevitable incompatibility of positive but organically separate blends of ego, initiative, and socialization, it is crucial to establish at least the implication of a second format. "Das braune Mädchen" is, after all, not a naked savage when she is first met with;

and her subsequent comportment is clearly not asocial, even if seemingly peculiar to her new acquaintances.

When the third encounter does occur, it again takes place in the context of a story hour on the old hazel root; that is, removed from the farm related activity of nutting. Having introduced all of the major ingredients of characterization and action, Stifter seems from this passage onward to maintain his thematic variation relentlessly beneath the narrative surface. The farm children will continue to represent a harmonious development of their particular amalgamation of ego, initiative, and socialization. The brown girl will be revealed increasingly as a representative of an alien world whose lower peripheries overlap the upper limits of its more materially advanced but less naturally integrated existential neighbor. The interaction of these innocently open young children is normalized from the standpoint of their respective spheres, as it is played out for the next several paragraphs in the physical setting of the nut mountain—the topographical symbol for the intersecting limits of their two worlds. The continual presence of the central figure of the nature-society amalgamation, the grandmother, and the absence of other alien figures preserve the neutrality of the mountain, for it represents neither of the two worlds completely.

The incipient tension in the narrative situation appears to be enhanced by the note of stylistic ambivalence in the narrator's attempts to explain the strange girl's fascination with her new acquaintances: "Es mochte wohl hinsehen, da es selber nicht die langen blonden Locken, sondern kurz abgeschnittene schwarze Haare hatte" (236). Is the obvious desire of the brown girl to observe the sensorially appealing aspects of her "discovery" as spontaneous as the affection of the farm children for their mica and "Katzensilber," or is it motivated by a burgeoning, critical self-awareness as suggested here? The answer is probably both. The red ribbons mentioned earlier seem to support the latter view, but the remaining, independently positive descriptive details of her appearance seem to support the former. She becomes more sociable and demonstrates her own physical beauty with her brilliant smile. She shares in listening to the grandmother's tales, and instead of fleeing when the farm party descends the mountain, she accompanies them downward in a manner which is actually summative of the thematic content of the entire passage: "Da man fortging, lief es nicht so eilig davon, wie die zwei ersten Male, sondern ging auch langsam auf einem Wege, der den Kindern nahe war, den Berg hinunter . . ." (236). And yet, the very next and final line of the paragraph re-evokes the ambiguity of the "mochte wohl" which began it: "Es hatte immer die nämlichen Kleider an, die es das erstemal angehabt hatte." One has to consider here whether this brief but pointed reference to clothing expresses an intrinsically negative aspect of the brown girl's characterization. There is a direct reference to the first description of her garments, but that depiction was neutral. And there is also the question of whether the farm children themselves are not attired in essentially the same nutting "uniforms" described on two earlier occasions (223, 226). A possible solution to this problem can be found in the more specific, later description of the girl's garments as the "schönes Gewand" ["beautiful garment"] which is ruined in service to the farm inhabitants (243). But is there an artistic discrepancy here which necessitates this nonsequential approach to analysis? The answer, apparently, is that there is not; because it is quite probable that the author intends the ambiguity to be perceptual rather than actual. The observation and description of the brown girl at this juncture in the story must represent the viewpoint of her companions. And because of the already established supramaterial bond between her and the other children present, we could assume that any potentially negative or at least ambivalent perceptions of her would have to come from the grandmother. This venerable lady, being the primary representative of farm existence, would be the logical register for impressions indicative of a contrast with it. As this analysis progresses, it should become ever more apparent that the principal narrational impetus in "Katzensilber" derives from the increasingly strong impulse on the part of the brown girl to accept a transcultural socialization in the manner of Sture Mure. By the same token, the crux of the novella's thematic interplay variation will center on the paradoxical dilemma, that her capable initiatives mark her as a successfully initiated member of a separate existential format. When she herself achieves sufficient maturity to realize she has chosen a course of action which will lead to a destruction of her native identity rather than to a satisfying social integration, she too will have to flee in tears back to her origins.

In addition to the thematic associations between the two paragraphs which describe respectively the first and third encounters with "das braune Mädchen," there is also the larger structurally duplicative connection provided by a series of shorter, action-oriented paragraphs which follow these longer descriptive ones. Stifter's condensed imagery in these brief passages seems to further the immediate narrational and ideational complex, suggest thematic links with characterizations and situations from the first lines of the novella, and foreshadow the later conflict. The pointed though brief reference to the father, in the first paragraph following the lines quoted above, is a good example of such compositional coherence: "Der Vater erlaubte den Kindern gerne, daß sie auf den hohen Nußberg gingen, sagte aber, daß sie dem fremden Kinde nichts zuleide tun sollten" (237). The father has already been characterized as the chief architect and engineer of the farm-nature amalgam. It is also apparent at this point that he is quite active in both the middle and lower strata of the vertically presented existential arena—on the farm and, in the wintertime, in the lower-lying cultural periphery represented by the capital. Yet, he has been conspicuously absent from the activities at the upper topographical limits of his world. Stifter usually presents thematically significant foreshadowings which occur in the earlier and middle stages of his works in a suspensive, barely perceptible way. But there always appears to be an image, phrase, or even a single word which makes the point. Here, the father's implied ambivalence toward the higher-lying environs of his property could be glossed over as simply a respect for the rights of ownership. (He does not, in fact, own the Nußberg, as he purchases acreage on it only later in the story.) And his encouragement to his children to enjoy the upper regions could be seen as a natural parental desire for healthy recreational activities for his children. But his incongruous admonition that his well-behaved children should do no harm to their exotic new playmate can be seen upon reflection, and once again from the critic's vantage point of repeated readings, as another foreshadowing of the novella's essential thematic variation as well as of its tragic resolution. Also indicative of an impressive artistry is the fact that even such a powerful prefiguration as this one may be is achieved with a single, subjunctively expressed clause, the content of which could also logically be ascribed to a familiar parental utterance. One is reminded again that Stifter's pronouncements in his famous "Vorrede" to *Bunte Steine* on the artistic value of the commonplace is not a mere outburst of rhapsodic humility, but rather a genuine *Weltanschauung* about which he is serious and one which he is capable of implementing in his literary productions.

The other short paragraphs which bring this passage to a conclusion go on to complete the picture of a harmonious, as yet unthreatening "semi-integration" of the brown girl with her newly discovered interactional context. She is friendly but still mute and content to observe and listen. She now routinely follows the farm party's descent to the edge of the shrubbery. When she appears with a nutting rod similar to those of the other children, she holds it proudly aloft as if to demonstrate her enjoyment at "fitting in." It is assumable that she did not possess one earlier, although she was ostensibly on the mountain to gather nuts also.[3] It seems also that she is capable of more natural and physically demanding harvesting techniques, such as tree climbing. She seems to express, then, a growing willingness to integrate more fully. At the same time, she conveys a wish for reassurance when she finally makes physical contact with "Blondköpfchen" during a descent from the mountain—she gives her a gentle touch with her hazel rod. At this point, however, Stifter seems to suspend the potential for socialization across boundaries and leaves it at the upper limits of his physical setting. This suspension not only aids the general development of such interaction as a vehicle for the tragedy that ultimately occurs, but more specifically it prepares for a thematically critical development which takes place in the next narrative segment. The two final short paragraphs of the passage continue the now established routine according to which the brown girl participates in the activities on the Nußberg. She shows herself to be comfortably attentive to the grandmother's anecdotes and is affectionately accepted by her youthful peers, but she also maintains her essential alienness even within the midst of the imagery of assimilation. The children bring her gifts of toys and apples but place them near her in the grass in deference to her lingering wariness. Her reaction is expressed with a reflexive prepositional object which conveys the idea of a practical bonding, but from an apparently egocentric orientation: ". . . und es nahm dieselben und steckte sie zu sich" (237). Finally, there is a further intimation that the girl comes from another realm which is supportive of her. Hitherto it has seemed that she did not comprehend the spoken overtures of the farm group, but now she registers an understanding of the grandmother's stories, as evidenced by her variegated facial expressions. Even if she is a very fast learner, she must have had some form of tutelage from others to be capable of following such extended oral discourse. This subtly expressed but critical aspect of the brown girl's characterization is confirmed, along with other allusions to her possible provenance, at the very end of the story.

The temporary deemphasis of the central plane of the novella's structural verticality, the farm proper, continues on for several more pages despite a notable leap forward in narrated time. As already stated above, however, these passages bring a crucial element of the work's thematic variation to the foreground, in the context of which the middle stratum of the narrative's physical setting will gradually reassert its importance. The hailstorm section in "Katzensilber," as this particular group of passages can conveniently be called, begins innocuously enough with a pair of lyrical paragraphs depicting another idyll on the high Nußberg. While repeating a known pattern of action, Stifter expands significantly his thematic foundation. Nut gathering has become inconsequential at this point, the nuts having all fallen. The days are shorter, necessitating an earlier departure to the lower region, and the fact that it is now late autumn naturally evokes images of the annual descent to the capital. The fields below in lateral proximity to the house are, contrastively, still in a stage of productivity, being already plowed and showing the first green of the winter wheat crop. Yet, there continues an attachment to the upper limits among the characters: "Die Kinder saßen wieder auf dem hohen Nußberg, das braune

Mädchen saß auf einem Stein (237). The weather itself seems to participate in a nonseasonal beguilement, but there is also an incipient tension in the hyperbole of "ein gar heißer, schöner Herbsttag, wie kaum seit Menschengedenken einer gewesen sein mochte." In this paragraph the figures of the grandmother and the brown girl, representatives of different spheres of socialization, are portrayed positively within the idyllic scene but on separate ends of another natural image with ambiguously tensive overtones. The detail of the red ribbons on the brown girl's clothing is also strangely suggestive of a sovereign, potentially problematic energy such as fire or lightning. Even in "hanging" they are filled with power and they are reminiscent of the mountain sprite's portentous red jacket:

> Es war ihnen wohl, in der späten, Warmen Sonne sitzen zu können. Die Züge der alten Frau waren beleuchtet, die Steine glänzten, an den Zacken und Hervorragungen hingen gespannte silberne Fäden, und die roten Bänder des braunen Mädchens schimmerten, wenn sie die Sonne an einer Stelle traf, und sie hingen herab wie glühende Streifen. (238)

The thematically duplicative anecdote told by the grandmother this time introduces negative elements into the agrarian format with which the farm society is historically and topographically associated. In the time of the peasant wars, a courageous countess fends off from atop high castle ramparts a peasant rebellion. Her absent nobleman arrives in the nick of time and scatters the incendiary-minded rustics like a storm wind ["wie ein Sturmwind"]. This image of an idealized human relationship preserved as by a natural force, although it perhaps prefigures a later rescue scene in "Katzensilber," seems ironically distorted by the actual, parallel events in the outer narrative. The ramparts of the legendary castle are immediately reimaged in the growing wall of clouds which merge with the mountains to tower over the now glowing fields below. The tension continues to mount in a series of short paragraphs which alternate further images of the children at play, the gradually more ominous weather conditions, and the grandmother's increasing alarm at their situation. The use of the subjunctive mood, often the mode of ambivalence, increases notably towards the end of the passage, adding another element of suspense. It seems to tinge the positive simile of molten silver derived from the still partially gleaming clouds with ambivalence, as it does the grandmother's ironic dismissal of the possibility of a storm at this season. Mention of the brown girl's posture is, however, contrastively forthright: "Das braune Mädchen sah auch nach den Wolken." The grandmother continues to assess the worsening situation using the indicative, while formulating positive prognostications in the subjunctive. Her ambivalence is also mirrored and augmented by the balance of positive and negative natural portents which surround her (239). Thunder is heard, but it is weak and intermittent; there are trees for cover, but they may draw lightning; lightning flashes become visible, but the accompanying thunder is still distant, "als wären sie hinter den Bergen"; the clouds are now a dark wall, but the Nußberg is still illuminated with sunshine. The farm children adopt an untroubled attitude based on their previous experience of storms and the calm model presented by their parents in such circumstances. The brown girl displays neither the reflective ambivalence of the grandmother nor the uncritical confidence of the other children; she busily scours the vicinity for a place of refuge. Her eyes are no longer on the clouds but are directed downward to find a sheltering root tangle ["Wurzelgeflecht"] or small hole (240).

An important thematic point appears to be evolving out of the three different reactive patterns in this passage. The logistical aspect of the farm existential format is brought forth in the grandmother's anxiety over the distance between her party and the sheltering farmhouse; and thus, the tenuousness of the amalgamation of humanity and nature at the upper physical limits of the farm is also felt. When the grandmother prefaces her proposed solution to the crisis with a reference to religious lore, one is again reminded that the interaction of the farm society with its physical environs has become routine and part of a culturally institutionalized pattern. This aspect of socialization is perhaps more strongly developed in a character such as the grandmother, a self-proclaimed "country girl" whose life-long activities have centered on participation in the amalgam of farm and nature. Were she more like her son, the "engineer," with his more objective grasp of the existential mechanics involved in their lifestyle and a less pronounced attachment to its religious formulae, she might be able to concentrate on the highly unseasonal but nonetheless recognizable signs of the coming hailstorm. In other words, because of habitualized patterns of activity solidified by the passage of many years, she appears to have lost to some degree the ability to adapt to unique situations. If she herself senses this fault, her reaction is to refer to the most sublime of those habitualized patterns—the religious one. The children continue to be less aware of the approaching danger, even though their youthful egos should respond more directly to the immediate situation. This is probably because of their hitherto positive role as liaisons between the world of the farm and of the high country of their mysterious playmate. They possess both the institutionalized confidence of their parents and the eagerness for new experiences of the brown girl, neither of which attitudes creates any instinctive sensitivity to the problematic events. "Das braune Mädchen" is, by contrast, a being whose interaction with the natural world is of a continual and direct kind. A spontaneous ability to perceive and deal with the vagaries of natural forces would have to be a social premium in the implicitly more physically exposed and less institutionally controlled existential realm from which she assumably hails. The reversed positive-negative polarity of this established thematic contrast continues throughout the passage, showing the representatives of the farm group in an ambiguous though not unsympathetic light, while the representative of the other realm will be depicted in terms of active and unquestionable positivity.

The directness of the positive characterization of the brown girl here is initiated by the structural juxtaposition of a single sentence, declaring first that she has left the scene and then that she immediately returns carrying bundles of branches which have been collected for winter heating needs. This logistical detail appears on consideration to indicate another instance of the author's technique of compositionally evolving and consolidating his thematic intent.

It is of course reasonable that such materials would be commonly present in a rural environment. But would it not also be reasonable that there be some completely natural provision for the brown girl's superior initiative? The absence of the sought-for "Geflechte" or "Holung" allows the girl's initiative to succeed not solely because of her alien capabilities, but because she adapts elements of the farmstead existence. One is again mindful here of the ability of that other alien figure, Sture Mure, to improve upon the methodologies of her adopted world.

The brown girl's cheeks glow with her efforts to construct a shelter from the limb bundles, a sign of ego-generated energy highlighted by the limited action of the other characters, who are settling into a hazel thicket for refuge. Significantly, she lapses into her native tongue and must resort to the energetic device of sign language to warn the others to escape the coming hail by entering her shelter. The position of the lean-to is in the same downwind location where the grandmother wisely sought a protective thicket, but the older character from the farm society quickly recognizes the individually superior initiative of the exotic child and quickly removes the other children to the safer haven. The brown girl positions herself at the outermost limit of the enclosure, an action which fits her role as initiator of the arrangement. It is perhaps also a sign of her emerging status as an outsider who effectively serves the conventional society, but who must constantly exert a personal initiative to be in touch with that existential sphere.[4] She seems for the moment content with holding onto Emma's blond locks as a reward for her efforts, so her psychological orientation apparently is still one of a childlike appreciation for the novelty and possibilities of human interaction.

While the depiction of the human representatives in this section of "Katzensilber" shows the amalgam of farm and nature in an ambivalent light, the description of the hailstorm reveals how destructive that nature can be (242). A plethora of verbs expressing violence, such as "fassen," "umlegen," "jagen," and eight variations or derivatives of *schlagen*, conveys in the space of a single paragraph the utter desolation of the upper reaches of the farmstead.

And the only actual reference to the farmhouse grounds proper in this description is a subjunctively equivocal simile, which implies similar disruption at the lower elevations. It in turn is immediately followed by a contextually associated declaration of the practical impossibility of any equal human initiative. The final image of the paragraph is the somber description of the destruction of the party's original refuge. The section of text reads:

> Das Laub wurde herabgeschlagen, die Zweige wurden herabgeschlagen, die Äste wurden abgebrochen, der Rasen wurde gefurcht, als wären eiserne Eggenzähne über ihn gegangen. Die Hagelkörner waren so groß, daß sie einen erwachsenen Menschen hätten töten können. Sie zerschlugen auch die Haseln, die hinter den Bündeln waren daß man ihren Schlag auf die Bündel vernahm. (242)

The next paragraph confirms the fact that the catastrophe is widespread, affecting the entire region. Only "weiche Dinge" can withstand the onslaught of the myriad hailstones, things such as the sheltering bundles and the persons cowering beneath them in a terrified unity of basic humanity. The brown girl's initiative has saved their lives, but the remnants of the grandmother's hazel thicket "machten, daß Wind nicht in die Bündel fahren und sie auseinander werfen konnte" (243). The anxious prayers of the grandmother during the storm suggest a divine ordination of this instinctive socialization across existential limits, and the storm begins to diminish with a downpour which seeps through the covering bundles to baptize the little congregation of the new human collective.[5] But there are already faint hints of separately reestablished orientations when the party crawls out from their shelter as the rain passes. The brown girl instinctively looks down to check her valued companions while the grandmother, perhaps feeling more complex responsibilities, looks first to the skies to make sure of things. As the children exit, they are again named but in reverse order as though their individualities must now reintegrate with their former base of identification, the farmstead society. The brown girl has been cut on one of her exposed arms by a hailstone but she modestly discourages the attentive sympathy of her companions. Here Stifter reevokes a complex of images which have contributed to and continue to sustain the development of his thematic vision. The "arms" motif can be traced back to the Sture Mure episode (226), and it seems significant that the brown girl should be injured just there in her successful attempt to preserve from harm her companions from the conventional world. The clothing of all the players is soaked, as was already allowed for in the earlier, optimistic predictions of the grandmother; but only the lovely garment ["schönes Gewand"] of the brown girl has been soiled to the point of ruin. She is depicted as capable of such productive sacrifices, and this must be due in part to her less materialistic background which is perhaps less encumbered with institutionalized trappings than is the conventional society. At the same time, it seems quite natural for the grandmother to carefully gather up her charges' baskets and pouch and assist them carefully on their homeward descent, "damit sie sich beim Fortgehen an sie anhalten und ihre Kleidchen aufheben konnten" (244). Hence, the clothing motif continues to be symbolic not of egocentrism, but of an integration with an identifiable socialization complex.[6] The brown girl accompanies her friends downward; this is expressed in a brief declaration which seems to accentuate her independence: "Das braune Mädchen ging mit ihnen." The contrast Stifter provides here of the grandmother's detailed preparations for the descent—which reflect her amalgamated existence—with the brief, self-assertive initiative of the brown girl appears supportive of the thematic variation involving separate and ultimately incompatible formats for the dynamic interplay of ego, initiative, and socialization.

The destruction of the upper reaches of the farmstead by the storm highlights the formalistic aspect of that zone's material orientation, evident in the grandmother's attention to material organization so soon after the real life-and-death initiative of the brown girl. There is now a clear choice for the brown girl. She can either return to her own existential sphere or she can involve herself in the life which goes on below, as there is for the time being no longer any "middle ground." Her decision to accompany her friends in their descent to the farm provides another narrative and thematic foretaste of what will transpire in the remainder of the story. Her simple attachment to the novel but intuitively sympathetic social context she has encountered on the Nußberg will cause her to gradually direct her personal initiatives more and more to an understanding and adoption of the existential core of that context—the world of the farm. In terms of the larger structural arrangement of "Katzensilber," the author is finally completing an extended "vertical" segment of his narrative, which began with the first appearance of the brown girl. By the end of this segment, the overall dynamics of characterization and plot propelling the story to its final thematic conflict and resolution will be outlined in full. From that point onward, the remaining events, interactions, and images will continue to cyclically develop, embellish, and intensify the tragic potentiality of the tale. To achieve this compositional consolidation, Stifter must continue to present the farm society positively and at the same time construct a narrative substratum that begins to anticipate the inevitable failure of that lifestyle to fully assimilate an intrinsically sympathetic agent from another realm. The stormy disruption of the idylls on the Nußberg appears to be the point of departure for a series of paragraphs which continue to present "das braune Mädchen" in positive, altruistic terms. But the already established positive features of her farm companions begin to restore the earlier balance. The grandmother is again her actively protective self, and the children show their characteristic curiosity and acceptance of natural phenomena, even amidst the wreckage of the storm-battered landscape. They carefully observe the details of the damage and stop to examine some of the hailstones which so lately threatened their lives. The balance then swings back again to another superior initiative of the brown girl when she locates the now submerged footbridge across the swollen meadow stream. It is interesting to consider if the impersonal "man" is used in this context to perhaps absolve the figure of the grandmother from blame for her nearly ineffective initiatives (245). A positive focus seems to be kept on the extraordinary nature of the alien girl's actions, with no explicit detriment to the guiding figure from the other realm. The balance then wavers once again, as the brown girl's arrival steady and sure ["fest und sicher"] at the far bank ["das jenseitige Ufer"] is contrasted with the grandmother's subjunctively tentative and then successful duplication of the feat. It is also interesting to note that the central object of this particular scene, the little stone bridge, is a product of the father's initiative, the principal creator of the farmstead format. Hence, the general trend towards regaining a positive image of the farm society continues to be balanced with ambivalent details. A major thematic strand of the plot, the evolving commitment of the brown girl to socialization across existential boundaries, appears also interwoven with this technique of ambivalent evaluation. One indicator of a changing orientation to her new society is the fact that she now concentrates on caring for the boy Sigismund, instead of continuing to court the attention of the blonde Emma.

Sigismund, the already established symbol of a harmonious integration of contrastive attributes under the aegis of the farm amalgam, will become more and more a beloved encouragement to the brown girl in her own quest for integration.[7] Sigismund intuits this incipient bonding when the brown girl reaches for him to bring him across the brook. He releases the hand of his grandmother, his former source of individual security, and puts himself in the hands of the alien girl. Thus, he fulfills his role as a liaison for assimilation from the other realm, an assimilation which the brown girl approaches with quiet responsibleness. She carries him safely across the rising waters and enters another world (245). But as is to be expected, Stifter sets even this significant thematic prefiguration in balance. The practicality of the brown girl's initiative, along with its thematic significance, seems highlighted by the fact that the grandmother is physically less capable of carrying the boy while also tending to his sisters. It is also true that an urgent, timely collective effort is needed to make the crossing. This latter consideration is forcefully realized when the party looks back to see the waters have risen still higher, covering the few remaining vestiges of familiar natural phenomena and leaving in their stead "fremde, schwarze Dinge." Incredibly, the brown girl appears to share in this image of the dissolution of familiar natural signs, since two sentences earlier she is described in a different way—as "das fremde Mädchen" instead of the usual "das braune Mädchen." At this point Stifter again augments the point-counterpoint of his evaluative imagery with vertical spatial references (246). In a paragraph duplicating in structure and content the one depicting the initial stage of their descent, the storm refugees must embark upon a temporary ascent to the evergreen wood, before the final downward leg of their return to the farm. The passages involving the isolated interaction of the brown girl and her Nußberg companions at the upper limits of the farmstead are temporarily suspended here, but Stifter seems to maintain the thematic presence of that interaction continuously. Using neutral phrasing, he contrasts what will be the brown girl's last initiative for a while with the effectively reemergent and altruistically positive initiatives of the grandmother. It is also interesting to observe in this context how "ascending" becomes an ambivalent action because it is motivated by the desire to avoid things:

> Sie gingen nun auf dem Rasen aufwärts gegen den Wald. Sie mußten den weichen Haufen von Schloßen ausweichen . . . sie mußten den Wässern ausweichen . . ., und sie mußten den Bächen ausweichen . . . . Daher mußten sie öfter von einem Steine auf den andern springen, um fortzukommen, und öfter durch ein fließendes Wässerlein gehen. Die Großmutter ließ ihre eigenen Gewänder dem Wasser und dem Schmutze der Erde preis, um die der Kinder zu wahren und zu helfen, daß die kleinen leichter fortkommen konnten. Das braune Mädchen ging mit. (246)

The grandmother has herself gone beyond the stage of merely tolerating wet clothing and occupies the supraegoistic position previously assumed by the brown girl when she ruined her garment in serving her friends. It is interesting to note here, however, that unlike the brown girl's sacrifice, which was directed solely at preserving life, the grandmother is also concerned with preserving the protective cultural formulae represented by the clothing. The order of verbal elements in the penultimate sentence of the passage quoted above, with the protection of the clothing preceding the facilitation of the homeward trek, may indicate the inseparability of the farm-amalgam existential mentality and a materially manifest socialization. When the children are in fact returned to their home and mother, the reaffirmation and resanctification of the family nucleus by the farm society will take place in a spiritual and religious atmosphere. But a material orientation for the reestablishment of the farm-nature amalgamation as an integrated existential plane is also anticipated in the intervening scenes of the "rescue" by the father and his implement-toting helpers. A thematic recapitulation at the end of this entire segment of the novella would seem to portend that this indigenously evolved existential complex of human, material, and cultural elements—which is representative of the universal interplay of ego, initiative, and socialization—will present at least a substantial challenge and quite possibly a tragic identity crisis for the young individual from another realm who will soon seek to interact more closely with it.

When the father and his farmhands come from the woods to greet the grandmother and children, they bring dry clothing as well as ropes and other implements of rescue. The clothing, although a logical adjunct to the rescue gear, is not used, even though the children are soaked to the skin. Propriety, one of the institutionalized values of the conventional society of the farm, assumes a priority here as another indication of the inseparability of survival and its culturally evolved patterns. In fact, the father's first utterance upon glimpsing his dearest kin sums up the cultural, familial, and logistical web which supports his entire world. He exclaims, "Da sind ja die Kinder, Gott sei gedankt, sie leben. Mutter, wo habt Ihr sie denn geborgen?" (246) The grandmother responds with an ironically brief allusion to the bundles of firewood and with no mention of the brown girl. The sincerely concerned but almost platitudinously expressed exchange of logistical information and reassurances continues with no mention of the critically important role played by the brown girl. The two youngest farm children come forward in their wet clothing and greet their parent, "wie sie es am Morgen vor ihrem Frühmahl zu tun gewohnt waren, und küßten ihm die Hand." The elder daughter refrains in deference to the presence of the other men, "weil . . . das sich hier nicht schicke." The subjunctive verb here almost seems to suggest the irony that under these critical circumstances it most certainly would be proper. At any rate, these images clearly convey the determination or perhaps even the instinct of this little society to preserve the evaluative patterns of the framework of socialization supporting their existential sphere. There is also a declaration of the necessity to continue to the center of that sphere, the house itself. In thematic terms, this appears to be in the interest of reestablishing the social core represented by the farmstead. The children cannot be cared for individually on the heights but must be hurried home to their mother, the chief symbol of the cultural base. The grandmother by stating that even as a girl she was inured to long periods in wet clothing contrasts herself, as a mature example of the traditional farm-nature amalgam, with the still maturing young egos of the children and their broader cultural connections with the world outside. During this developing reassertion of the farm's societal aspect, "das braune Mädchen," with the irrevocable worth of her recent initiative still vivid in the reader's mind, has assumed a posture of cautious disassociation: "Das fremde Mädchen stand in der Ferne, wie es sonst an dem Rande der Haselbusche zu stehen gewohnt war, aufrecht und steif" (247). The contrast here with the solicitous treatment received by the farm children, together with the use of the now infrequent alternate attributive "fremd" and the attitudinally connotative terms "aufrecht" and "steif," are apparently intended to maintain the thematic variation in "Katzensilber": the positive sovereignty of separate formats for socialization and the potential antipathy between them.

The imaginal reconsolidation of the farm society, provided by the scene of the family members closely encircled by the farmhands, reforms into a hierarchical progression towards the farmstead, with the family members leading the way. The brown girl remains in the background and again her participation in the dramatic events on the Nußberg gets only cursory notice. There may also be an additional, implicit ambivalence in the mixture of indicative and subjunctive verbal moods when the author continues the conversation between the grandmother and her son during their homeward descent: "Sie erzählte ihm nun, was sich auf dem Nußberg begeben hatte, und wie sie bis zu der Stelle gelangt seien, an der er sie gefunden habe" (247). There seems a suggestion in this stylistic arrangement that all the events at the mountaintop, both good and bad, can be incorporated under the aegis of an independently operative phenomenalism, within which the exotic nature of the brown girl could also be accommodated. But the initiatives subsequent to the action the party took on the mountain top to save itself have been increasingly oriented towards reestablishing the conventional culture of the farm. This process has been achieved structurally through the logically correct but also thematically supportive activity of the descent. And yet, there have been persistent reminders of the ironic nature of this procedure as a continuing echo of the deeper thematic concern in "Katzensilber." Stifter now seems to present the farm-directed activities in an ambiguous light to communicate both the paradox of antithetical positivities and also to elicit a sympathy for the intense logistical involvement of his conventional characters. This latter possibility seems well supported by the imagery of disruption which concludes the downward progress of the group. As the rescue party and family members pass through the previously familiar environs during their return to the farm, the magnitude of destruction elicits in the reader an empathy which almost but not quite balances the still perceptible absence of the novella's central figure. When the mother is described as a flgure in white rushing toward her family through the wet and ruin of the physical center of their world, to meet them at its formal limits at the corner of the greenhouses, it appears that this person who most embodies the cultural base of the farm society can provide the impetus for a new beginning—a beginning which can fully accommodate even worthy ones from another realm (240).

Her reaction is intense and quite different from those of her husband and mother-in-law. She brushes aside any logistical considerations with a desperate joy when she replies to Sigismund's apology for having brought back no nuts: "aber dich selbst du kleines unvernünftiges Kind . . ., das mir lieber ist als goldene Nüsse." She is intent only upon the living kernel of her existence. She has already credited her husband and God with this miracle, and pulling the children to her she reasserts the integrity of their individual selves by crying out their names. These reactions, as natural and moving as they are, once again underscore the intentional absence of the other child involved, the brown girl. Then, the open declaration of her part in the wonderful events is barely begun before the process of reestablishment again postpones it. The mother asks not to be reminded of the dire possibilities of what might have been, and the father limits himself to a schematic mention of the life-saving wood bundles before encouraging the family to move inside where the children can be properly cared for. The farmhands are released with gratitude by the parents and with the announcement of a celebratory "Feierabend," complete with a gratis portion of wine for all. The foreman, as senior representative of the laborers, expresses the thematic significance of this socialized "communion" when he replies, "wir haben nichts Besonderes getan, als was unsere Schuldigkeit gewesen ist" (250).

The reappearance nearby of the brown girl is depicted almost in the nature of an afterthought: "Das braune Mädchen stand in einiger Entfernung im Garten." Such a perspective is possible only after the farmhands have been dispersed, allowing a view of the path the party has just descended—an image rife with underlying remembrances of the alien child's critical and determinant initiatives during the catastrophic storm and in its aftermath. But the literal "distance" of the girl from the group in this scene begins to be supported by a perceptual one. The purpose of neglecting her in the preceding narration seems to be brought out in the attitudinally connotative, negative expression "nicht beachtet" [not noticed], and it was the obscuring mass of the farmhands which separated her from her living liaisons to the farm world. Her shy and hence ostensibly unsocialized behavior was assumed in part responsible for her imagined absence. The author indicates that even the farm children contribute unconsciously to the isolation of the brown girl in this passage. For when he describes how they drop their mother's hands and rush happily to the side of their young friend, he tells us that it is "das fremde Kind" they perceive standing there in "their" ["ihrem"] garden. The perceptual ambiguity seems to continue in the passage as does the subjunctive mood, when the father finally relates to the mother, "daß es das braune Mädchen von dem hohen Nußberg sei, und erzählte ihr, was es heute zu dem Schutze der Großmutter und der Kinder getan habe." Any chance for a more balanced social reorientation under a loving impetus from the mother is suspensively bypassed, and Stifter has the father, the most pragmatic and hence least alterable exemplar of the conventional farm mentality, make the official overture to the brown girl for an integrative relationship. She, for her part still uncommitted to such an arrangement, flees back to the upper regions of the landscape. When a farmhand offers to give chase, the father supports his children in a total prohibition of force, but he offers a thematic summation of the entire narrative up to this point and an ironic foreshadowing of its tragic outcome when he expresses the following scenario:

> . . . das Mädchen hat meiner Mutter und meinen Kindern heute den größten Dienst erwiesen. Darf man es überhaupt nicht rauh behandeln, so darf man es jetzt um so weniger, so lange es sich nicht schädlich erweist. Wir werden es schon . . . zu finden wissen, . . . und wir werden die Art schon finden, wie wir . . . ihm sein Leben vielleicht nützlicher machen können . . . . (251)

"Das braune Mädchen" has reacted to the father's offer by fleeing like a stag ["wie ein Hirsch"], giving some justification to the father's subsequent assessment of her as a forest creature which can fend for itself in the natural world. But it is a vertical reference which expresses the positive and perhaps even superior nature of this character; her refuge is "die höchste Höhe" ["the highest height"]. The pervasive ambivalence of the farm society in regard to the brown girl appears tonally supported by the almost exclusive use of the subjunctive mood in stating concern over her wound, and narratively by the father's conviction that the best possibility of socially integrating the girl is that she be left to her own judgement ["Ermessen"] in this matter. The implication is that she will come around eventually. Ironically, the father has intuitively recognized the maturity and effectiveness of the brown girl's initiatives but has failed to pursue his observations to their logical conclusion. The brown girl is, of course, precocious in her physical and mental handling of natural contingencies, which are no doubt an integral part of her world. But she is not a wild beast, for she must have acquired her survival ability along with her pretty garment in some other sphere of socialization. It should be remembered, however, that life was not normally a "moveable feast" for Stifter and his contemporaries, and sharing one's way of life was really tantamount to an encompassing, integrative commitment. The father has offered what he sees as a genuine boon to the girl.

The thematic focus of the novella continues to alternate between passages depicting the conventional farm society and those depicting critical, often tersely expressed initiatives of the brown girl. At this juncture, which is almost exactly the half-way point of the story, it can be said that the essential compositional and thematic elements of "Katzensilber" seem to have been clearly established. They are for the most part only artistically embellished and philosophically enhanced from this point onward. Thus, it can also be said that from the analytical viewpoint there is a basic similarity of structural and philosophical interaction in "Granit" and "Katzensilber," in that both are concerned with the narrative exposition of positive formats for socialization. And although the scope and complexity of that exposition is much more extensive in the latter work, due chiefly to the complicating factor of the brown girl's alternate world, an acceleration of the analytical process similar to that effected for the latter part of the chapter on "Granit" seems permissible at this point. The present analysis will, then, in a like manner now concentrate on the relationships between broader segments of the text and the ways in which they lead to the resolution of Stifter's thematic variation in "Katzensilber."

The last passages analyzed above depict the brown girl's first descent to the farm and actually end with a lengthy depiction of the farm society's inner workings (252-55). Images of the careful nurturing of the children subsequent to their traumatic experience at the upper physical limits of their world are combined with religious and practical assessments on the part of the elders, as to the meaning of these events within the culturally defined parameters of their collective existence.[8] The resultant dual resolution which they propose takes the form of a conviction to continue to rely ultimately upon divine dispensation, but it also includes a plan to purchase land on the Nußberg for the erection of a sheltering hut. The pattern of interaction of the farm society with its natural surroundings is again evident in the admission by the practically-minded father that the eventuality of another such cataclysm is remote, but that he will nonetheless build the structure forthwith. The brown girl's presence in these deliberations is limited to a brief reference to her as a divinely arranged occurrence sent to preserve the faithful and to instruct through the revelation of her person. The reader may perceive that this revelation involves the problematics of socialization across existential limits, but Stifter leaves the point open within its immediate context and moves ahead to the next cyclical segment of the narrative. That section begins, not surprisingly, with the plans for and the actual rebuilding of the farmstead. The father's first directive concerns the restoration of the greenhouses, the recognized spatial boundary of the farm proper, and only then does he initiate the repair of the house itself. The fruit trees, primarily a luxury item, come as a third priority. This sequence seems to imply a psychological defensiveness against outside influences, as well as an attempt to reestablish controllable alternatives to purely natural resources. Importantly, the father only afterwards seeks information on the brown girl, beginning with the conventionally socialized institution of the local church. Ultimately he must question the local hunter, however, whose wide wanderings make him privy to almost every coming and going in the area. The information the latter character supplies, however, is only of a general sort, emphasizing once again the significance of the upper topographical limits of the novella's physical setting for the apparent thematic dichotomy of separate social and existential forms:

> Es seien Banden gewesen, sagte er, aber sie seien immer in den höhern Wäldern, die gegen Bayern hinüberziehen, gewesen und hätten sich längs des Saumes angehalten, an dem sie durch die Länder gewandert sind. (257)

Although this passage is one of only two direct indications of the girl's probable ethnic origins, the choice of indirect reportage with its subjunctive mood again seems to connote ambiguity. This suspensive technique has already been shown to occur frequently with Stifter, and it almost always points toward an important reiteration of theme. The example quoted above is no exception, and the ambivalent tone here suggests that the father is not prepared to consider an indigenous existential source for the problematic character of "das braune Mädchen" to be socially valid in a conventional sense. His initial investigative efforts end unsuccessfully as a terse declaration shows: "Der Vater kehrte unverrichteter Dinge wieder heim."[9]

Stifter has the father continue the quest for information. After an intervening description of the continued rebuilding of the farm, on the first sunny day after the storm he accompanies his daughters and son and mother to the Nußberg for the first time. He openly declares his intentions in regard to the brown girl when he says, "Er möchte sich ihm dankbar beweisen" (258).

The subjunctive verb form perhaps again intimates the failure of this initiative, which in fact repeats itself "mehrere Male." But the ironic balance of images continues when the father uses the opportunity to do restorative work at this upper limit of the amalgamation sphere. Aided by his girls, he returns the mutely evocative bundles of firewood to their proper places. This action seems to be for him on at least an equal footing with his efforts to construct an integrative relationship with the Gypsy girl. The girl, for her part, indicates by her absence a continuing unwillingness to openly cross over the social limits from the other side. When the father finally desists from his Nußberg visits, the girl comes forth immediately; and there is a wonderfully expressive solidarity combined with an acceptance of individualities in the way the farm children gingerly touch the brown girl's arm and ribbons, as she strokes the contrastively colored locks of both girls and holds the boy's hand. This image seems to represent in miniature an ideal dynamic balance of ego, initiative, and socialization. And there is even evidence in her sudden ability to speak German understandably of a growing inclination in the Gypsy child to adopt the ways of her friends. The implication of some at least educationally tolerant home environment in this last detail is, however, quickly rendered ambivalent by the observable disrepair of the child's garments. Hence, as Stifter has initiated another cycle of ascents and descents within his physical setting, so too does he begin anew the thematic balance of positive and negative or at least ambivalent tonalities in his imagery and characterizations. Along with this balancing he continues the forward narrative momentum, which represents a general technical similarity between "Katzensilber" and "Kalkstein." But the pivotal difference will prove to be that the narrative technique of "two steps forward, one step back" in "Katzensilber" is not used to justify egocentricity as a permissible element of socialization. The process appears to be used in "Katzensilber" to clearly define a positive, if conventional form of socialization on one hand, an individually worthy but culturally alien ego on the other, and the differences which separate them. Such a relationship must eventually require the permanent absorption of the exotic by the conventional, or the rejection of the conventional by the exotic. In other words, Stifter will continue to depict first a system where ego-generated initiatives are gently controlled and directed toward the consolidation of a tentative amalgamation of nature and society, and second an exemplar of a system wherein the assertive initiatives of the ego are given priority as the best social solution to a constant and direct exposure to the vagaries of nature. The collision course of these two existential dynamics is given form in the narrative and thematic weave of "Katzensilber."

As the story continues, the farm children continue their outings to the upper regions. But they go now expressly to visit their friend, and she in her turn begins to accompany them to the symbolic limit of the farm proper, the "Glashäuser." This convivial arrangement reestablishes an ideal microcosm of socialization on the mountaintop at the same time it alludes to the ongoing reestablishment of the farm society below. In reading this passage one may recall Stifter's statement in his "Einleitung," where he specifically uses the terms "bunte Steine" and "Katzensilber" in describing his affinity for mineral specimens and their aesthetic significance for him (18). Hence, the words of the title receive our special attention when he writes:

> Sie brachten dem braunen Mädchen schöne Sachen. Das braune Mädchen brachte ihnen auch bunte Steine, es brachte ihnen verspätete Brombeeren, es trug in seinem Wamse Haselnüsse herbei . . ., oder die gefleckte Feder eines Geiers oder die schwarze eines Rabens. (260)

In its total context, it might be said that the ideational dichotomy represented by these images, were its parts mergeable, could well symbolize the apex of Stifter's mature artistic vision—at least at the time the collection of novellas was published. It would require a special study of all six novellas to ascertain conclusively Stifter's rationale for the title of his published collection. But within "Katzensilber" this allusion to pretty stones is evocative of the mica motif, which earlier represented the innocent acceptance of natural beauty regardless of its material value. The narrative traverse of the novella's vertical physical setting continues, but this time with the harmonious society ["Gesellschaft"] of the nut mountain becoming ever more connected to farm society. The brown girl still stops at the greenhouse limits, but there is no longer any stiffness in her demeanor as she exchanges friendly caresses with her playmates before departing. She is integrated figuratively with the household existence of the family when the children argue over who likes her the best, and the parents pay careful attention to the grandmother's comments concerning the girl. Even the invariable routine of the wintertime city sojourn seems imbued with the spirit of their new friend as the farm children lament the extended separation, "als ob ihnen ein tiefer Schmerz und ein tiefer Kummer angetan worden wäre" (261). But this reaction expressed in the subjunctive is followed immediately by a positive description of the charms of the city, the space most antithetical to the upper world of the brown girl. The children's sorrow lessens, the further downward they travel enroute to the capital, until they become completely enchanted by the novel sights of urban existence. Stifter again uses the thematically charged motifs of clothing and glass panes ["Glastafeln"] effectively here in his reference to the shop windows, to reassert the oppositive positivity of the cultural and formal base for the sojourning farm society. Thematic balancing through the use of the clothing motif continues when the family returns to the hill country, and the growth of the children is measured by the need to alter their garments. "Das braune Mädchen" has grown also; but her clothes have not been altered and they highlight again the material aspect separating her from the conventional world. And although her hair is longer and worn in a style more like that of her conventional companions, her naked arms hang close to her sides, as if to insulate her ego from its own vulnerability to the affectionate attentions of her companions (262). These images appear to have a divided narrational significance, which again suggests the dualistic nature of the thematic variation. There is an apparent willingness on the girl's part to imitate her conventional friends, yet her physical maturation implies an inevitable juncture when she must commit more completely to this adaptation. The critical question is, will this accomplished ego, capable of such valuable initiatives, be able to effectively maintain its dynamism within a form of society so materially and culturally different from that which must have formed it? The answer at this point seems to be yes, so long as only the flexible parameters of a child's world are in effect, making the only significant center of human interaction the activities and joys shared among similarly innocent companions. This ideal but temporally limited existence continues to develop in "Katzensilber" as the brown girl adapts more and more to her adopted surroundings, ever more confident of the good will of her playmates and finally even in that of the farm society overall. But Stifter's narrative weaving-in of imaginal, structural, and stylistic intimations of the coming crisis seem always present.

The cyclical fall and rise of the rural landscape is quickly reestablished in two brief paragraphs following the children's happy reunion at the spatial limits of their respective worlds; and the psychological boundary persists as well, since the brown girl still stops at the greenhouses. There is also another indication that she is subject to a separate sovereignty; this is implied in the designation "häufig" to describe the frequency of her mountaintop rendezvous with the farm children who are there always ["immer"]. But there is a developmental expectancy evoked by the numerous images of new growth on the cultivated and natural planes, which manifests itself also in a thematically pivotal event in the human sphere. The amalgam of farm and nature revives through the combined agency of personified physical phenomena such as the sun, which lures ["lockt"] the green color back to the earth, and through the initiatives of the father—expressed in a more communal and less egocentristic form through the use of "lassen." As if in concordance with the expanded human harmony represented by the farm children and their exotic friend, nature bursts forth with a productiveness greater than usual. In this consummately positive context, the brown girl is finally brought into the physical center of conventional socialization:

> Einmal in der Fülle des Frühlings, da alles blühte und duftete und sich das menschliche Herz erfreute, . . . und man bis zu den Glashäusern gekommen war, hatte Blondköpfchen die Hand des braunen Mädchens gefaßt . . . (sie) sah dem braunen Mädchen ins Angesicht und sagte: "Komme mit, Komme mit!" (264)

It is the eldest, physically most dissimilar and, implicitly, the most socialized of the farm children who extends this earnest invitation. But it is Sigismund, the living symbol of integrative potential, who actually succeeds in bringing the girl forward. She proceeds through decreasingly natural contexts: from the trees, to the green garden, to the sandplot in front of the house, up the steps, and finally she stands on the parlor carpet. The grandmother discreetly leaves the room, as if aware of the psychological stress occasioned in the brown girl by her first exposure to the center of an alternate existence. The material alienness of her situation is evinced by her wide-eyed observance of the conventional material accouterments of furniture and domestic appointments. Yet she consumes trustingly the refreshments offered by the other children. She can find no fitting orientation to the toys she is shown, and the children turn to a display of their finest clothing. There seems to be a suggestion in this scene that her initiatives may become subordinate to her appreciation of artifacts symbolic of the farm's institutionalized basis. The incipient tension here is fully realized when the elegantly dressed mother inadvertently overwhelms the girl with her offer of preserved fruit, an apparently unfamiliar and suspicious commodity. The farm children are quick to mollify the situation with demonstrative gestures of affection, and when the girl takes her leave, the narrative returns to the vertical traverse which now routinely includes happy interactions at both its upper and middle foci. Once again, an intervening passage of concordant natural burgeoning leads into a narrative event of thematic import when the father begins construction of the promised shelter on the Nußberg (265). Stifter, however, again seems to slow the forward momentum of his narrational-thematic complex by depicting an ambivalence on the part of the brown girl toward the father's building activities. The brown girl mutely observes the construction of the hut along with the other children, but she is conspicuously absent when they fete their father, the engineer of this miniature house at the uppermost limits of the farmstead (266).

The brown girl does join the Nußberg society again when only the children and grandmother are present, but the frequency of these reunions is designated by "whenever" ["wenn"], in contrast to the "always" ["immer"] which describes the children's attendance in the hut. The subconscious antipathy of the brown girl, who had to ["mußte"] go along into the hut is eventually complemented by the farm children's own return to an exclusive interest in the natural patterns of their hilltop playground. They resume their stone gathering and they rest on the old hazel root as if the playhouse no longer existed. This childlike enthusiasm for the indigenous treasures of the upper regions is balanced, however, by a more frequent and effective integration of the brown girl below in the setting of the farmhouse. Ironically, the children leave their hilltop retreat earlier now, because their friend routinely comes home with them to their dwelling and associates with them there for longer periods. The mother has adopted the strategy of dressing and coiffing herself in the manner of her daughters in order to allay the girl's shyness, and she always sequences her offers of food to serve the brown girl last. By these devices she successfully utilizes the child's already formed trust in the other children to gradually accommodate her to the broader socialization format to which she is being exposed. There is still consideration of the girl's sensitivity to too great an alteration in the native state of her physical and psychological constructs, or ego. This is manifest in the style of the new garments given her, which are "wie das frühere war . . . " (268). But the addition of decorative embellishments and half-length sleeves imaginally maintains the movement toward a conventional domestication of this child—a process which could prove unnaturally limiting, however well-intentioned and protective its impulses. The glowing and capable arms earlier alluded to several times will now be partially covered for convention's sake.

The father embarks upon his second round of initiatives on behalf of the brown girl, which takes the form of another, perhaps more determined search for her origins. But although he goes higher and higher into the surrounding countryside, even beyond the limits of his property, he obtains in the end only contradictory and ambiguous statements from those most marginal of all social participants, the pitch distillers (269). Again Stifter seems to enhance this thematically important ambiguity by use of the tonally connotative subjunctive mood in the context of indirect discourse. "Das braune Mädchen" herself remains silent when queried gently by the mother—an attitude which should surprise no one who has heard of the traditional secretiveness of the Gypsy folk. The problematic obscurity of the girl's roots is immediately contrasted, however, by her initiative towards an even greater social assimilation, for she now comes to the farm alone and of her own volition. She silently observes the home tutelage of the farm children and quickly and unexpectedly approximates their academic abilities. She is encouraged in this and finally carries her inclinations toward "transsocializing" to the point of indulging herself in a more conventionalized posture of childlike dependency: "Wenn die Großmutter mit den Kindern fortging, hing es sich so gut an die Schürze derselben wie die anderen Kinder und ging mit" (269). The incongruity of this image is clear when one remembers the consistently capable initiative the girl has exhibited in even the most traumatic circumstances. It is apparent the child is responding to an irresistible opportunity to be exactly that: a child, and with a sheltering socialization context which allows for a gentler process of ego development than does the austere world from which she comes. Yet her attachment to that world must still be strong, as she will in nowise consider overnighting at the farm. Other reminders of her former self-sufficiency also are evident as the vertical narrative traverse ascends for the last time to its upper spatial limits, "auf den hohen Nußberg." The format of this particular outing focuses again on the farm related activity of gathering hazelnuts. The brown girl again demonstrates her desire to participate productively by having fashioned for herself or obtained from somewhere a long stick with a hook at one end for pulling down the higher branches. Yet the very precocity of this initiative, in comparison with those of the other children who are still equipped with their less formidable hazel rods, sets her apart. When she agilely swings up into the branches to facilitate the harvest, she is still markedly "das braune Mädchen."

She comes from a world separate from that of the farm but similar enough in one aspect of its natural logistics to have occasioned a spontaneous interaction on a basic human level. The unproblematic, non-threatening union of sincere childlike natures at the topographical limits between two cultural and ethnic existences must now recede gradually into the narrative background, as Stifter begins to complete the exposition of his thematic variation and its tragic resolution. The happy search for pretty stones and the convivial solidarity at the hazel root give way to detailed images of preparation for the imminent winter season. When this narrative segment ends with the descendent motif of the seasonal pilgrimage to the capital, the brown girl's growing involvement with the socialization format of the farm is preserved by Sigismund's parting gifts to her of his toy trumpet and his picture book—both conventional possessions for a child.

The winter visit is drawn out somewhat this time, implying a suspensive highlighting of the brown girl's position back at the farm. There is also a simultaneous reenforcement here of the sympathetic integrity of the family and employees who form the nucleus of that conventional society (271). It is observable in this regard that the leave-taking actually took place in two chronological stages. The first had the children bidding a tearful good-bye to the brown girl, the second depicted the equally touching farewell of the son to his mother with the maids and farmhands looking on. The homecoming is equally dichotomized, because the long winter has also logically separated the snow-bound farm from the unnamed seasonal haven of the brown girl. The grandmother is fine, as are the maids, the farmhands, and even the animals. But what of the Gypsy child? Stifter does not prolong her reappearance here, as he has several times before; instead he has her come to the house this time to greet the homecomers. This act appears to summarize the results of an interim stage in the thematic development. "Das braune Mädchen" has transferred her main point of contact with her conventional associates from a neutral physical setting at the natural topographical limits between their world and hers to the social center of theirs. There are still some counterbalancing traces of her sovereignty of character, such as the fact she has grown taller and lovelier with her raven mane of hair longer and fuller than ever. And her assimilation of the social interplay of the farm seems at this point still to have connections with the more natural world of her provenance (272). The shared learning and play of all the children is depicted in the same paragraph through natural images of plants and birds, whose self absorbed trilling and soaring may remind the reader of the positive but highly individualized early initiatives of the brown girl herself. Her course seems set though, as Stifter leaves her momentarily poised on the brink of a complete integration with the other world, even into the logistical realities which form the base of its cultural structure: "Das braune Mädchen war nun auch nicht scheu, wenn der Vater bei den Kindern war, und es wich vor den Knechten und Mägden nicht zurück, welche im Hause, im Garten und auf den Feldern herumgingen und arbeiteten." When he returns her to the story some eight pages later, it is to depict her penultimate initiative. The courage and integrity of that action will ironically bring about her final tragic attempt to socialize herself across existential boundaries, in the interest of a chosen human bond but at the expense of an innate one.

The catastrophic event which impels "Katzensilber" toward a narrational climax and thematic resolution is similar in the strength of descriptive imagery to the earlier hailstorm. One summer evening when the father is away on business and after "das fremde Mädchen" has taken her customary leave for the day, the eldest of the farm children persists in the assertion that she smells something burning. A fire has indeed broken out in an adjacent hayloft and quickly engulfs the entire farm complex, including the residence. The mother and children call to each other by name, instinctively consolidating their family group, and hurriedly gather critical papers and belongings in their flight from the building (273). But the mother's instinctive initiative to preserve the most precious extensions of her own ego, her children, while at the same time salvaging the documents important for the material maintenance of the farm unit, presents with even greater force than the hailstorm passages the practical inseparability for the farm inhabitants of human bonds and socialized patterns. The forced division of the mother's initiatives has nearly fatal consequences, for in the flurry of action Sigismund, the beloved boy, is trapped on the upper floor of the burning house. After the mother frantically directs herculean but futile efforts by the farmhands and neighbors to clear a way into the flaming structure, she falls to her knees in a prayerful supplication for the boy's rescue. At this moment the brown girl dramatically reappears as if by divine ordination:

> In diesem Augenblicke tönte ein gellender Schrei: "Braunköpfchen, Braunköpfchen!"

> Und ehe man sich's versah, huschte eine dunkle Gestalt gegen das Haus und kletterte wie ein Eichhörnchen an dem Weingeländer empor und war in dem nächsten Augenblick durch das Fenster verschwunden.
> Alle vergaßen ihre Arbeit, oder was sie immer im Herzen hatten, und richteten ihre Augen auf das Fenster.
> Es dauerte nicht lange, so kamen zwei Gestalten am Fenster an . . . Es war das braune Mädchen und Sigismund. (280)

The references here to the "dunkle Gestalt" ["dark figure"] and an "Eichhörnchen" ["squirrel"] seem to reevoke the characterization of the brown girl as a saving natural force, like the dark flower in the grandmother's earlier religious assessment of the hailstorm crisis. These images also highlight once more her natural physical precocity.

Stifter avoids crossing over into the realm of melodrama or sentimentality and maintains his serious thematic intent by limiting the success of the brown girl's heroic initiative, almost as she implements it. She has brought Sigismund out of the inner passageway where he was trapped, but she is unable to bring him onto the vine trellis in order to complete the rescue. Amid shouts from the spectators to tie sheets together, the foreman and another farmhand push through the crowd bringing ladders. These implements along with the farm wagon to which they were attached have escaped the conflagration, "aus Gottes Vorsicht und mit dem Willen der Frau . . ." Thus, the author underscores again the bisection of two social dynamics which creates the thematic variation in "Katzensilber." The initiative of the mother as a fully established agent of the farm existence has been needed to complete the rescue. The self-sacrificing effort of the brown girl, however, was necessary to initiate the process. The outcome is a happy one, as Sigismund is helped down the ladder by his beloved friend. But there is a consistent exoticism in the depiction of the girl: "Als sie auf dem Grase waren, kniete das braune Mädchen auf seine eigenen Fersen und sah den Knaben mit den schwarzen Augen an" (281). And there seems to be an even more thematically significant ambivalence in the isolated use of the subjunctive mode to describe how her joy may have been perceived by the farm society: "Man hätte in der dunkeln Nacht und bei dem Scheine des Feuers sehen können, wie diese Augen freudesprühend waren, daß er gerettet sei" (281). The tension of this relationship continues, as the sheer magnitude of the effort directed against the inferno and towards removing the children from further danger renders the temporary neglect of the wonderful brown girl at least understandable. Her critical participation in the events is reiterated, as it was in the hailstorm passages, retrospectively several paragraphs later; and her absence is again rationalized on the basis of her former pattern of never staying at the farm past nightfall (284). But there is irony in the fact that only after a temporary existential base is set up in the greenhouses—the symbolic limit of the central farm socialization format—is there any time for even considering the well-being of the brown girl.

The possible underestimation by the farm dwellers of the brown girl's commitment is highlighted by her sudden appearance in the garden at daybreak, indicating she may have been close by through the night. Her social impulses are, however, still centered on basic human bonds of love and individualized acceptance and only peripherally active within the institutionalized material and cultural contexts of her adopted world. The conflict this orientation will create for her in the world of the farm seems again ironically foreshadowed in the subjunctively expressed intention of the father and mother to raise "das braune Mädchen . . . und es demjenigen Glücke zuzuführen, dessen es nur fähig wäre" (287). There is no blame to be placed in this paradoxical misunderstanding between representatives of two essentially positive human formats—one individualized and inherently ego-motivated and the other collectivized and intrinsically societally motivated. Both pursue fulfillment with sincerity, energy, and good will.[10] But the inevitable failure of their union is brought to a narrational climax in the closing three pages of the novella. The farm family's necessary preoccupation with maintaining the physical base of their cultural existence appears to render them incapable of committing to a full integration of someone from beyond that format, unless they can assume a social superiority to justify their effort. They seem to assume, from the ironic viewpoint of the conventional third person narrator, that the brown girl begins to stay overnight at the house because her new clothing makes such a situation more acceptable to her. Stifter juxtaposes this view in the same sentence with a statement that she comes often of her own accord to be with the children. The "new" clothes are, in fact, the second such set provided for her and are cut like her originals, as were the first set given her. It is for love and admiration of her playmates that the girl will try to enter their world and emulate their ways. The clothing motif, though centrally symbolic for the farm family, represents only one more compromise for the brown girl. This becomes critically evident when it is taken to its logical extreme and she is eventually induced to wear conventionally feminine garments. She loses the psychological equilibrium she has so laboriously constructed for her new existence, as well as her native athleticism, and becomes "scheuer" and takes "kürzere Schritte" (288). The additional assumption by the farm society of parental neglect, as a rationale for expecting no resistance in their plans for the girl, also seems to be rendered subtly questionable by the structural arrangement of one subjunctive verb structure in the midst of several indicatives. The assumption is made that anonymous parents have allowed the girl free reign in the region, have never come forth for an introduction, have seen the gift clothing, and have known "daß das Kind oft in dem Hause sei" (288). Even without any express attention to the choice of the subjunctive, these actions as a whole could be seen from an objective viewpoint as quite proper parental postures, considered in their own cultural context. There must be a greater premium on the individual ability to adapt to one's surroundings quickly and effectively in such a mobile and fringe society as that traditionally ascribed to the Gypsies. And like her narrational and, as it finally turns out, her genetic prototype Sture Mure, the brown girl pursues her cross-over socialization initiative faithfully and effectively for several years. She applies herself assiduously; and she even appears to absorb the basic tenets of the Christian faith, along with all the other activities and skills developed by her foster sisters. But the fact that she can in no way be induced to accompany the family to the city and remains through the winters at the farm indicates that her adaptability has reached its limits. (Here one must wonder where she spent all of the previous winters, as one wondered where her nights were spent before her gradual integration with the household. The several implications throughout "Katzensilber" of an at least tenable home environment for her, such as her original garments and her gradual mastery of German, are a subtle but essential part of the thematic exposition.) The final failure of the girl's entire endeavor appears once again to be intimated in an understated but seemingly pointed usage of the subjunctive. The hope is uttered of continuing to bind her to conventional society "bis sein Herz von selber in dem Hause sein würde, bis es nicht mehr fortginge und sein Gemüt ohne Rückhalt hingäbe (288).

The intuited inhibition ["Rückhalt"], however, is something as inborn and unavoidable for the brown girl as her admirable willingness to serve those she loves. As Clementia, Emma, and Sigismund reach advanced adolescence, they all show signs in their individual actions that they are in complete harmony with the process of socialization which they are undergoing, and they work to consummate it. The girls each develop their own particular type of beauty and lovability, and Sigismund becomes a paragon of handsome young manhood. The increase in culturally oriented social activities during this epoch at the farm points to the potential of marriages for the three. It is during one such afternoon entertainment, with local and city guests, forfeits, and music and dancing, that the brown girl makes her final break with the farm existence. She has waned physically as the others have bloomed; her once glowing cheeks are now sickly and her shining gaze has dimmed. The stress of her conflict has apparently been building for some time, and now that the activities of her peers have confronted her with her own maturity, she realizes with a breaking heart that she must find her way back to the world where her own future lies. That future must start with a personal initiative to preserve the social continuum of which her birth, her formative years, and even her ethnic identity are a part. The father and mother find her weeping, oblivious to her fine clothes, in the sand beyond the greenhouses as they too seek a respite from the gaiety in the farmhouse. The mother seeks to reassure her and tells her she is as their own cherished daughter. But in the same breath she betrays her uncertainty about the girl's orientation as she offers the resources of the farm world to the anonymous parents if they still live. The brown girl replies sobbingly, "Sture Mure ist tot, und der hohe Felsen ist tot" (290). Thus she highlights her pathetic isolation, and at the same time she reveals the connection of her own story to that of the earlier-treated character whose failed attempt at integration helped establish the work's thematic pattern. And indeed a thematically relevant revelation is contained in the simply stated disclosure of her parentage. The existence of a positive alternate format of socialization for the girl is finally declared here. Thus she explains her own physical and psychological base of support and, most importantly, the origin of both her impulse to transsocialize and her eventual realization of the impossibility of its success. She has no doubt learned much from her mother about the other world—knowledge which she has put toward becoming a part of it. But her mother's final lesson is one she must now sadly confirm in her own fate. In the scene which terminates her physical presence in the narrative, her beautiful hair, consistently suggestive of an innate positivity, is contrasted with her "nicht mehr so voll und glänzende Arme," a symbol of her diminishing initiative effectiveness. She fiercely caresses the mother in response to her sincere assurances of total acceptance, but her uncontrollable tears bedew the lady's beautiful gown. Then, when she perceives the silent weeping of the father, she must recognize as he does the impossibility of living fully in two separate worlds.[11] She flees back to her heights, never to be seen or heard from again. The father, as chief exemplar of the commitment and material effort necessary for a successful existence within a given society, has rightly been the one to share a final, silent understanding with the brown girl. And it is as the heir to this insightful position that Sigismund many years later stands upon the heights, back to which his childhood friend had flown. He hopes with a still aching heart that "dem Mädchen nur recht viel Gutes in der Welt beschieden wäre" (291). This closing line of "Katzensilber" refers most likely to the old world of the brown girl, to which she returned with the pain she had found in the new one of conventional society. There appears to be, however, a final exposition of the thematic variation here, in the concept of two separate worlds and the hope that their truest values are somehow transferable. The figure of Stifter's brown girl thus proves to be representative of a simple but profound variation of his thematic interplay, and in nowise is she merely "ein schwer erziehbares heimatloses Zigeunerblut."[12]

The solitary vigil of Sigismund which closes the longest and perhaps most thematically complex of the novellas in Stifter's *Bunte Steine* is reminiscent of that of the mother in "Granit," who gazes out over her world at that story's end from the vantage point of age; and it is also similar conceptually to the last scene of "Kalkstein," with its lone graveside visitor lost in the contemplation of a departed "saint." But the variation of the thematic interplay of ego, initiative, and socialization which Stifter formulated in "Katzensilber" is neither a confirmation of the societal bedrock of family and community, nor is it the necessity of seeking illuminated worth in the gray, sometimes shadowed "limestone" fringes of society. It is rather, Stifter's artistic perception of the simple beauty and value of indigenous human personalities. They can, like "Katzensilber," shine and sparkle within the perimeters of their natural milieu, but they can also tragically diminish to dull, diaphanous trifles when extracted from it. Human beings are sovereign phenomena which together produce the light of humanity, but their separate energies may be elementally and perhaps divinely evolved to sustain only limited contact with each other.

NOTES

1. Sjögren's assessment of this particular activity as "obsessive" (361) seems to overlook the agrarian coherence in Stifter's description of the farmstead.
2. For a concise analysis of this motif see Le Hoven 13-20.
3. For an interesting insight into the folkloric significance of this implement see Mason 116-17.
4. There appears to be little justification in this scene for Eve Mason's assertion that the girl is deliberately crowded out by the grandmother, 121.
5. Oertel Sjögren describes this scene similarly as a "baptism into a nobler state," 368.
6. Le Hoven also discusses this motif at length, 13-20.
7. At least one critic goes so far as to see this passage as the beginning of a full-blown, romantic love relationship. See Le Hoven 41-47.
8. One perceives the intentional incompleteness here of what the "Vorrede" nonetheless touts as the highest integration with nature: the mind (cf. "Vorrede" 6-7; also Aluf 107).
9. It is difficult to understand the reluctance of some critics to accept the Gypsy origin of the brown girl, in view of Stifter's wide travels in his native Bohemia, a traditional stronghold of this race (cf. Mason 128, Sjögren 362).
10. Both Mason and Le Hoven have recognized the evaluative equality of these two worlds, but they still assign to the brown girl a predominantly non-human symbolism.
11. The mute but touching communication expressed in these lines of the story seems to refute Mason's comments about an emotional deficiency on the part of the farm family and a disappointment in them on the part of the girl. See Mason 123.
12. See Walter 9.

Chapter V

Conclusion

THE FOREGOING MATERIAL has attempted to contribute new analytical and evaluative insights to the still problematical understanding of Adalbert Stifter's well-known collection of novellas, *Bunte Steine*. Having first identified a central interpretive question in the secondary literature as a search for some clearly discernible, thematic and/or compositional common denominator which would unite the members of the collection, this study has subjected three representative works from that collection to an intensive and extended structural and stylistic analysis. The conceptual point of departure has been that of a broad-based thematic interplay, involving the universal human dynamics of ego, initiative, and socialization. While various critics have described the separate manifestations of these thematic elements in the individual novellas, they have also cited the need for more detailed studies demonstrating an underlying artistic coherence and unity for *Bunte Steine*. The present study has taken up that task by combining a philosophically broad critical orientation with a protracted but detailed textual analysis.

In the process of developing this interpretive model for *Bunte Steine*, particular attention has been given to the author's varied arrangements and prioritizations of the common compositional elements of structural and contextual juxtaposition and to the stylistic choices of connotative language and grammatical modalities. The result of this approach has been a demonstration of three distinctive variations of the common thematic interplay of ego, initiative, and socialization, each of which stands in reciprocal compositional relationship to the narrative structure of the novella in which it is expressed. In "Granit" the thematic interplay is presented in the context of multiple time frames, separate characterizational complexes, and a basically circular narrative progression. The sum of those elements provides for an exposition of the thematic interplay in its basic, positively resolved form as the bedrock of human life. In "Kalkstein" the dynamics of ego, initiative, and socialization are principally centered upon and extracted from a single, concentrated, but still ambiguous personality in order to demonstrate the necessity for an evaluative flexibility within the social context. Hence, the compositional movement is fittingly linear in "Kalkstein" to form a tonally subtle, or "limestone-gray" specimen of the thematic aggregate. In "Katzensilber" the problematic potential of the universal interaction is expanded to include the concept of dual existential formats, each essentially positive within its own logistical determinism but tragically limited in its capacity for lasting interaction with the other. The vertically structured physical setting and narrative action of this tale form a proper compositional environment for the notion of an intrinsic good, which like its mineralogical symbol, however, must remain within its organically conditioned milieu to maintain its native luster.

The three variations of a common thematic interplay discussed here, while in and of themselves remarkable evidence of a fertile narrative virtuosity, are perhaps even more significant as proof of an underlying unity for stories which to this point appear to have eluded any fully satisfactory critical subsumption. And possibly of at least equal importance is the development in this study of an analytical methodology which could be equally effective in an even more extended format, encompassing detailed analyses of all six of the novellas in the collection. Such a basic but comprehensive study might provide an additional link between what Boeschenstein has designated as two principal tendencies among Austrian writers of Stifter's epoch: "an enlightenment which is complementary to the spacious sphere of baroque acceptance of a pluralistic world."[1] In regard to biographical studies on Stifter, there could be a resultant partial clarification, at least, of the ongoing ambivalence cited by Margaret Gump when she writes:

> ... we should not interpret his life and work retroactively ... as ... a bright superstructure above a dark abyss. We must understand him from ... his works ... and shall find that he was neither the serene man of childlike faith of the early critics nor the pathological figure of some recent ones.[2]

Stifter's artistic vision has as its ideational wellspring the irrefutable concept of man, the social animal; and that vision manifests itself in an inspiring literary variety created from the basic materials of human nature and existence and offered to us, for our appraisal and reflection, as a handful of "bunte Steine."

NOTES

1 Boeschenstein 102.
2 Gump 22.

Bibliography

Aluf, Israel. *The Concept of Integration in the Works of Adalbert Stifter.* Diss. Brown U., 1958. Ann Arbor: UMI, 1958. 5897634

Bertram, Ernst. *Studien zur Adalbert Stifters Novellentechnik.* Dortmund: Ruhfus, 1907.

Blackall, Eric A. *Adalbert Stifter: A Critical Study.* Cambridge: Univ. Press, 1948.

Bleckwenn, Helga. "Adalbert Stifters *Bunte Steine*: Versuche zur Bestimmung der Stellung im Gesamtwerk." *Vierteljahresschrift des Adalbert Stifter Instituts des Landes Oberösterreich* 21 (1972): 105–17.

Boeschenstein, Hermann. *German Literature of the Nineteenth Century.* New York: Saint Martin's Press, 1969.

Czucka, Eckehard. *Emphatische Prosa: Das Problem der Wirklichkeit der Ereignisse in der Literatur des 19. Jahrhunderts. Sprachkritische Interpretationen zu Goethe, Alexander von Humboldt, Stifter und anderen.* Stuttgart: Steiner, 1972.

Danford, Karen Pawluk. *The Family in Adalbert Stifter's Moral and Aesthetic Universe: A Rarefied Vision.* North American Studies in Nineteenth Century German Literature. New York: Peter Lang, 1991.

Dehn, Wilhelm. "Schwerpunkte des literaturkritischen Interesses an Stifter." *Literatur in Wissenschaft und Unterricht* 1.2 (1969): 118–35.

Geulen, Hans. "Stiftersche Sonderlinge: 'Kalkstein' und 'Turmalin'." *Jahrbuch der Deutschen Schillergesellschaft* 17 (1973): 415-31.

Gradmann, Stefan. *Topographie/Text; zur Function raümlicher Modellbildung in den Werken von Adalbert Stifter und Franz Kafka.* Athenäums Monografien: Literaturwissenschaft 96. Hain, 1990.

Gump, Margaret. *Adalbert Stifter.* Twayne's World Author Series. New York: Twayne Publishers, Inc., 1974.

Haines, Brigid. *Dialogue and Narrative Design in the Works of Adalbert Stifter*. London: Modern Humanities Research Association, 1991. xiii.

Hall, Murray G.; Renner, Gerhard. *Handbuch der Nachlässe und Sammlungen österreichischer Autoren*. Vienna: Böhlau; 1992. xxi.

Hermann, Carol Jane. "The Art of the Novelle, 1800-1855." DAI. 1989 Feb.; 49(8): 2210A-2211 A.

Hertling, G.H. "Mignons Schwestern in Erzählwerk Adalbert Stifters: *Katzensilber, Der Waldbrunnen, Die Narrenburg.*" *Goethes Mignon und ihre Schwestern: Interpretationen und Rezeption*. Ed. Gerhart Hoffmeister. California Studies in German and European Romanticism and in the Age of Goethe 1. New York: Peter Lang, 1993. viii, 165-97.

Hoefert, Sigfrid. "Realism and Naturalism." In *The Challenge of German Literature*. Ed. Horst S. Daemmerich and Diether H. Haenicke. Detroit: Wayne State UP, 1971. 250–61.

Konrad, Gustav. "Adalbert Stifter." *Deutsche Dichter des 19. Jahrhunderts: Ihr Leben und Werk*. Ed. Benno von Wiese. Berlin: Erich Schmidt Verlag, 1969. 366–86.

Lachinger, Johann; Pintar, Regina. "Adalbert-Stifter-Bibliographie." *Vierteljahresschrift des Adalbert Stifter Instituts des Landes Oberöstereich* 39 (3-4) (1990): 41-86.

Le Hoven, Susan Hylton. "Natur und Zivilisation in Stifters 'Katzensilber.'" M. A. Thesis. U of Tennessee, 1986.

Lo Cicero, Donald. "Stifter and the *Novelle*: Some New Perspectives." *Modern Austrian Literature* 1.3 (1968): 18–29.

Mason, Eve. "Stifter's *Katzensilber* and the Fairy-Tale Mode." *Modern Language Review* 77 (1982): 1–29.

Mautz, Kurt. "Das antagonistische Naturbild." *Adalbert Stifter: Studien und Interpretationen: Gedenkschrift zum 100. Todestage*. Ed. Lothar Stiehm. Heidelberg: Lothar Stiehm Verlag, 1968. 139-68.

Naumann, Ursula. *Adalbert Stifter*. Sammlung Metzler. Stuttgart: Metzler, 1979.

Requadt, Paul. "Stifters 'Bunte Steine' als Zeugnis der Revolution und als zyklisches Kunstwerk." In *Adalbert Stiftert: Studien und Interpretation: Gedenkschrift zum 100. Todestage*. Ed. Lothar Stiehm. Heidelberg: Lothar Stiehm Verlag, 1968. 139–168.

Roedl, Urban. *Adalbert Stifter in Selbstzeugnissen und Bilddokumenten, dargestellt von Urban Roedl*. Reinlek bei Hamburg: Rowohlt, 1965.

Rohlfing, Martha. "Stifter's *Bunte Steine* as a Cyclical Work." *Michigan Academician: Papers of the Michigan Academv of Science, Arts, and Letters*. 10.2 (1977): 197–205.

Sagarra, Eda. *Tradition and Revolution: German Literature and Society 1830–1890*. Literature and Society. New York: Basic Books, Inc., 1971.

Schoenborn, Peter A. *Adalbert Stifter: Sein Leben und Werk*. Bern: Francke, 1992. xviii.

Schröder, Hans. *Der Raum als Einbildungskraft des Dichters bei Stifter*. Frankfurt: Peter Lang, 1985.

Sengle, Friedrich. *Biedermeierzeit. Deutsche Literatur im Spannungsfeld zwischen Revolution und Restauration*. Stuttgart: Metzler. 3 vols. 1971-80.

Sjögren, Christine Oertel. "Myths and Metaphors in Stifter's *Katzensilber*." *Journal of English and Germanic Philology*. 86.3 (1987): 358–71.

Steffen, Konrad. *Adalbert Stifter: Deutungen*. Basel und Stuttgart: Birkhäuser Verlag, 1955.

Stern, J.P. "Stifter's Fiction: '*Erhebung* without Motion.'" *Novel* 1 (1968): 239–50.

Stifter, Adalbert. *Bunte Steine. Späte Erzählungen*. Sonderausgabe ed. by Max Stefl. Darmstadt: Wissenschaftliche Buchgesellschaft, 1963.

Swales, Martin. *The German Novelle*. Princeton: Princeton Univ. Press, 1977.

Swales, Martin; Swales, Erika. *Adalbert Stifter: A Critical Study*. Anglica Germanica. Cambridge: University Press, 1984.

Walter, I. E. Ed. "Hinweise." *Werke in zwei Bänden* by Adalbert Stifter. Vol. 2. Salzburg/Stuttgart: Verlag "Das Bergland Buch," 1958. 7–12.

Index

German entries in italics represent primary titles and untranslated terms. German entries in quotation marks represent secondary titles, quoted material, figurative usages, or terms analyzed linguistically.

abilities 58, 64, 123
Abwechslung 68
acceptance of world
    by Stifter 178
accumulation of connotations 117
accumulation of images 30
adjectival designation 132
aesthetic values 4
age of change 4
agrarian format 144
agrarian life 113, 133
agriculture 46
alien being 124
alien capabilities 147
alien child 11
alien ego 115
alien figures 126, 139
alien girl 137, 150
alien realm 123, 133
alienness 117, 143
"Allgemeine,
    das Ganze und" 19
alliteration 25
allusion 36, 59, 75, 79, 127, 129, 138
allusions 37, 123, 143
almanacs 1
alpine existence 130
alpine farmer 133
alpine origin 133
alter-ego 46, 123
alternation of paragraphs and
    passages 44
altruistic character 113
altruistic effort 104
altruistic initiatives 115
altruistic personality 88
altruistic service 105
altruistic terms 150
Aluf, Israel 12, 13, 110
amalgamated existence 133, 149
ambiguities
    editorial 1

ambiguity
    and reiteration 31
    and words 26
ambiguous characterization 67
ambiguous imagery 132
ambivalence
    critical 3
ambivalent imagery 89, 138
ambivalent symbol 80
ambivalent tone 82
amount of text
    for atmosphere 26
    for limiting initiative 37
analyses
    generalized 7
    individual 9
    of isolated passages 7, 14
analysis
    detailed 18
    line-by-line 5, 9, 16, 18
    of character 58, 68
    structural, stylistic 177
analytical focus 77
analytical methodology 25, 178
anecdotes 16, 44
anger 29
Angst 52
animal husbandry 46
annual bibliographies 2
antisocial behavior 47
antithetical models 104
apparel 118
appraisal of collection 179
appreciation of the collection 13
apprenticeship
    ethical 46, 101
approach to the collection 5, 177
aptitude
  commercial 6, 98
"arme Spielmann, der" 12
"arms" motif 148
Armut 93

art
  ideals on 4
  literary 9
articles 97
  longer 3
  recent 12
artistic choice
  and style 27, 30
artistic coherence
  and unity 177
artistic discrepancy 140
artistic instinct 31
artistic integrity 53
artistic naivete
  and style 40
artistic virtuosity 30
artistic vision 25, 179
assessment of initiatives 36
assets, family 104
assimilation, social 53
assonance 25
atmosphere 25
  creation of 26
  thematic 25
atmosphere-engendering passage 26
atmospheric preface 25, 31, 33, 59, 67
attire 62, 64, 71, 75, 76, 137
attitude
  ambivalence of 68
  and ego 42
  and personality 68
  integration 62
attitudinal correspondence 68
attitudinal indicators 78
attitudinal separation 66
audience 124
"Außenseiter" 110
austerity 133
autobiographical sources 54, 112

Bach 136
balance
  narrative 35, 88, 92
  of figures 72
  of images, structure, style 58
  of momentum, retardation 75
  suspensive 86
  thematic 35, 40, 44, 45, 48,
balanced imagery 115, 120, 128, 131, 138, 160
balanced paragraphs 116
Banden 159
baptism 175
baroque acceptance
  of world 178
basic materials
  of human nature, existence 179
battlefield 43
bedrock 174
  of human life 177
"Begrenzung des Geistes" 8
behavior
  patterns of 29, 119
  socially integrated 30
"Bergkristall" 1, 3, 9, 17
Bergland edition 17, 54
"Bergmilch" 1, 2, 5, 9
Bertram, Ernst 3
"Besiegung des Vitalen" 8
Bible 81, 87
biblical parallels 8
bibliographies
  annual 2
  end 3
Binnenerzählung 114
biographical interpolation 99
Blackall, Eric A. 5, 6, 7, 110
Bleckwenn, Helga 17, 110
"Blondköpfchen" 131
Boeschenstein, Hermann 3, 178
boldface 24
bonding 143, 151
book-length critiques 7
"Böse, das" 108
boundaries 115, 121, 129, 134, 136, 142, 151, 168
"braune Mädchen, das" 8, 113
"Braunköpfchen" 131
brown girl, the 5
brute egoism 42
building activities 164
"bunte Steine" 161, 179
burgeoning 164
Bürger 101
burial ceremonies 41

Index

business 6, 15, 40, 45, 98-104, 168

capacities
    of spirit, mind 58
causative 127
celebration 69, 71-73, 85, 86, 96, 98
certification 102
character appraisals 14
character constellations 23, 57, 130, 177
character development 69
characterization
    and ego 36
    and theme 25, 54
characterizational ambiguity 76
characterizational foil 73, 82
childbirth 99
childhood 98, 173
children's literature 1
child's delusion
    and style 25
Christian faith 171
Christian minister 81
Christian values 37
Christlike goodness, isolation 107
Christmas tale 1
chronological sequence 135
church 28, 53, 69, 71, 73, 80, 86, 96, 117, 159
church offices 42
circular narrative 177
citations 19
citizens 37
civil servant 61
civility 80
classical form 54
clauses 24, 25, 63, 79, 86, 88, 99, 24, 25, 118, 142
    and structure 24, 25
cleric 7, 15
"Cloth, the" 62
clothing 16, 26, 29, 33, 76, 118, 123, 130, 132, 137, 140, 144, 149, 152-154, 162, 165, 170, 171, 172
co-adoptee 11
cogency and concentration
    of theme 23

coherence
    and theme 30
    of collection 177
collection of novellas 177
    introduction and preface to 1
    philosophical base for 4
    unity of 4
collective effort 128, 151
collective egoism 74, 134, 131
collective existence 158
collective viewpoint 117
commerce 101
commercial aptitude 6
commercial function 38
commercial interaction 134
common compositional elements 177
common thematic denominator 2, 4, 17, 18
common thematic interplay 57, 69, 177, 178
communal acreage 80
communal initiative 42
communication 175
"communion" 156
community
    and initiative 43
    peasant 13
    spiritual 42
comparative, the 76
comparison 111, 113, 117, 136, 166
complacency 43
comportment 64, 139
compositional amalgam
    and theme 52
compositional coherence 141
compositional common denominator 177
compositional consolidation 150
compositional diffusion
    and theme 54
compositional lapse 73
compositional manipulation 11
compositional parallel 137
compositional techniques 6, 109, 112
compositional unity 115
compositional variations 109
compromise 171
    and theme 43

conceptual point of departure 177
confidence 145, 146
conflict 25, 30, 34, 111, 122, 141,
    150, 170, 1720
confrontation 93
congregation 42, 148
connotation
    negative 79
    positive 79
    contrastive 76
    orthographic, phonetic 69
connotative choice 6, 79, 85, 112,
    117, 154, 177
consecration
    celebration 72, 85, 98
    of graves 45
    of remains 51
continuity 132
    ethnic 7
    familial 23
contrast and comparison
    and theme 54
contrastive attributes 151
contrastive connotation 119
conversation 74, 84, 154
correspondence 11
    with Heckenast 9
    with L. von Eichendorff 12
    professional 10
courage 168
courts 134
critics 16, 137, 142, 175, 177, 178
    ambivalence of 4
    recent 8
criticism
    problems in 1
    survey of 2
crucifix 45, 81, 108
cultivation 115
cultural amalgamation 118
cultural base 118, 124, 135, 153,
    155, 162
cultural continuum 13
cultural formulae 152
cultural guidelines
    and initiative 52
cultural parameters 134, 158
cultural periphery 141

cyclical segment 118, 130

danger of critical method 25, 154
death 1, 6
degeneration 43
dehumanization 103
denouement 50
    and structure 31
description
    and contrast 50
    and frame narrative 45
    and style 36
    and theme 23, 26, 42
    as symbol 49
descriptive focus 65
destinies
    of humankind 8
determinant of individual development
    13
determinism
    logistical 178
development
    of poetic monotony 12
    of the individual 11
    of thematic interplay 23, 95
developmental view of Stifter's works
    13
dialogue 71, 74, 88
    and style 40
didacticism 5, 77, 94
    and theme 34, 44, 51
didactic purpose
    and narrative frame 48
didactic tone
    and narrative frame 45
    and style 40
differentiation of perspective 21
diffusion of thematic interplay 23
dignity 64
digressions 14
    autobiographical 98
diminuendo 89
diminutives 65, 78, 127, 129
direct discourse 71, 75
    and style 27, 40
    and theme 29, 32
direct quote 60, 74
disease 42

Index

distilling 38
diversity
    of tales 17
divine justice 5, 41
divine occurrence 158
divine order 37, 40, 45, 52, 58
divine temptation 47
doctor 96, 97, 133
documents 105
domestic helpers 33
double entendre 88
dreams 53, 102, 108
dual characterization 82, 84, 87, 94
dual existential formats 178
duality of motivation 28
duplication
    and theme 39
    textual 54, 73, 82, 87, 109
duties 98

earlier versions of novellas 12
ecclesiastical status 62
editorial ambiguities 1
editorial pressure 122
education 8, 84
ego 8, 18
ego-centered images 25
ego-centered initiative 27, 29, 48, 54, 128
ego-initiated conflict 34
ego-initiative-socialization interplay 60, 77, 99, 113
Ehre 72
Eichendorff, Louise von 12
"Einleitung" 2, 19, 161
Einzelgänger 71, 98
emotional deficiency 175
emotional response
    and theme 32
empathy 114, 155
empire 41
engineer 117, 141, 146, 164
English 86
enlightenment 178
entrepreneurs
    woodland 38
environmental expectations 98
epic 6

equilibrium 10
equivocation 62
Erstdrucke 110
"erzählerische Trick" 110
erzieherischen Motiven 17
ethical apprenticeship 46
ethical duties 49
ethical tenets 35
ethnic identity 159, 166, 172
evaluative imagery 151
evaluative orientation 67, 96, 153
existential base 149, 170
existential boundaries 115, 124, 129, 136, 140, 151, 168
existential "border-zone" 15
exotic child 147, 154, 163
exoticism 134, 158, 166, 169, 172, 173
experience-based assessments 84
exploitation of natural resources 50
expressive modes 69
extended family 119
extension of theme 42
extensions of ego 168
extra-narrative provenance 137
extra-personal responsibility 115

failure 37, 48, 62, 95, 103, 108, 150, 160, 170
    of ego 92
fairy tale 7, 16, 19, 115, 124
Faith, the 37, 42, 178
familial patterns 7, 23, 119
family 5, 15, 33, 42, 50, 98-104, 111, 126, 152, 162, 170
farm activity 120, 139, 166
farm amalgam mentality 152
farm community 128
farm-nature amalgam 136, 141, 154
fate 6, 152, 155-160, 163-165, 170
fault 46, 146
fear 51
Feierabend 43
festivities 63, 65, 72, 73
fiction 62
    approach to 9
figurative expression 42, 44
final sacrament 107

Index

final testament 105
financial contexts 104
fire
    punitive value of 16
first person 57, 72, 75, 107, 113
"fitting in" 142
foil
    character 73, 82, 94, 101, 109
folly 23, 28
forebears 98-100
foreshadowing 26, 89, 99
formality 80, 95
formative years 172
formulae
    cultural 152
    religious 146
foundation of human society 49
frame narrative 5, 54, 112
friendship 77, 79, 92, 94, 121
fulfillment 45, 53, 111, 124
function
    of art 4
funerals 100, 104, 107

garments 82, 140, 160, 162, 165, 171, 172
gatherings 62
Geist 8
Gemüt 172
genre 4, 19
gentle law, the 2-4, 7, 11, 13, 15
geographical affiliations 113
German 160, 172
German literature 14
Geschäftsleuten 99
Gesittung 55
gifted individual 58
gnome 10
goals 40, 108
God 5, 6, 46, 155
Goethe 12
good will 170
Gott 37, 41, 46, 47, 73, 95, 108, 153, 169
government 59, 93
grace 40, 52
grammatical modalities 25, 68, 31-41, 43-47, 52-54, 112

    choice of 177
grammatical phrasing 98
"Granit" 1, 4-7, 10, 13, 18, 61, 67, 75, 78, 109, 138, 174
greed 133, 143
Grenze 34
Grillparzer 12
"growing up" 120
Gründer 108
Gump, Margaret 2, 10, 12, 178
Gute, das 108
Gypsies 1, 111, 160, 165, 171, 175

Hausierer 24, 25
Hebbel 17
Heckenast 9
hereditary expectations 98
hierarchical socialization 119
high-low imagery 70
"Hinweise" 17
Hoefert, Sigfrid 2
"hohe Felsen, der" 7
home environments 102
home tutelage 166
homiletic 5
human advancement 118
human collective 148
human dynamics
    universal 177
human interaction 45, 115
human types 10, 114
humility 32, 142
husbandry 46, 100, 115

Ibsen, Henrik 12
"ich", the 59
icons 53, 134, 135
ideational complex 125, 141, 161
ideational wellspring 179
identity 28, 117, 141, 153, 172
idiosyncrasy 88
imagery 6, 40, 63, 70, 88, 98, 114-116, 120, 132, 141, 151, 160
imaginal blend 116
imaginal concert 85
imaginal contrasts 122
imaginal density 128

imaginal sequences 115
imaginal softening 80
imagination 109
impersonal constructions 25, 112, 115, 119, 127, 150
impersonalized images 25
inaccuracies
    critical 15
incompatibility 138
    with "gentle law" 15
incompatible worlds 119
independent clauses 86
indigenous personalities 174
indigenous society 134
indirect discourse 74, 165
individual, the 2, 11, 14, 18, 24, 43
infinitive construction 76
influence of political events 5
inhibition 172
initiative 23-35, 37-54, 58-62, 74, 81, 88-96, 98-105, 111-116, 118-125, 131, 147-150, 160, 171-174
inner narrative 5, 15, 49, 51, 114
instinctive socialization 148
institutionalized values 146, 153
insularity 123
integration 8, 12, 24, 31, 49, 62, 77, 88, 92, 102, 123-125, 130, 141, 151, 165, 170
integrity 88, 92, 104, 155, 167, 168
interest in novellas
    contemporary 2
interpolation 30, 60, 95, 99
interpretative principle 16, 26
interpretive model 177
irony 41, 68, 73, 94, 104, 131, 153, 170
isolation 66, 70, 99, 103, 122, 156, 173
isolationist views 76

jealousy 105
"Jochträger" 124
journeyman 98
"junges Deutschland" 4
juxtaposition 35, 84, 112, 124, 125, 177

chronological 44
    of images, etc. 51
    of paragraphs 25
    of passages, etc. 53
    of terms 15
    structural 6

"Kalkstein" 1, 5-7, 12, 18, 112, 136, 160, 174
"Katzensilber" 1, 3, 5-9, 11-13, 15-19, 109, 178
Klassik 8
Kleider 140
knowledge 173
Konrad, Gustav 3, 110
Kraft der Jugend 9

language 6, 14, 107, 147, 177
"lassen" constructions 112, 113, 116, 127, 163
law 102, 104
    "gentle" 19
Le Hoven, Susan Hylton 175
Lebensunterhalt 39, 40
leitmotif 89, 96
lifestyle 38, 48, 81, 92, 146, 150
limitations 57, 121, 126, 127
    critical 12
limits 40, 111, 113-118, 132, 135-137, 141-143, 151, 163-167, 171
line-by-line
    analysis 5, 9, 16, 18
line-by-line balance
    of images 28
linear narrative 61, 67, 73, 89, 109
literary merits of the collection 14
literary cycle 4
literature
    periodical 14
    secondary 16
Lo Cicero, Donald 15
logistics 146, 153, 166, 178
longer sentences
    for balance 63
love 99, 102, 105, 110, 115, 170, 175
lust 128

lyrical style 14, 143
majority viewpoint 58
"man" 112, 113, 116, 119, 150
manifestations of thematic 177
Mann, Thomas 4
"Märchen" 15
marginal socialization 124
marriage 50, 172
Mason, Eve 15, 16, 19, 175
maturity 50, 111, 141, 157, 162, 172
melancholia 10
melodrama 7, 169
mental gifts 84, 101
metaphor 19, 34, 39, 107, 121, 134
metaphysics 14, 19
method
    critical 9, 17,18, 147
mineralogical symbol 178
mingling of images 121, 128
mixture of descriptors 129
Modern Language Association 2
monologue 95, 105
moral values 4, 12, 16, 40
motifs 30, 50, 64, 71, 80, 91, 103, 123, 137, 148, 162
    clothing 16
    pedagogical 17
multiple time frames 177
Mut 97
music 172
mythical, the 19, 42, 114, 130, 134

naivete 40
narrated time 143
narration-in-narration 35
narrational cycle 126, 129
narrational development 113
narrational form 67, 120, 138
narrational-thematic complex 164
narrational variation 57
narrative digression 124
narrative focus 132
narrative frame 5
narrative past 44
narrative perspective 21
narrative present 44, 53
narrative sketches 130
narrative structure 120, 177

narrative substratum 150
narrative technique 160
narrative unity 115
    inner and outer 13
narrator 23, 31, 45, 51-53, 59-61, 70, 81, 90, 105-108, 139, 170
nations 2
native identity 141
natural psychology 104
natural resources 50, 132, 159
natural sciences 8
natural wisdom 84
negation 79, 93
    of initiative 52
    of thematic 115
negative attributes
    of ego 26
negative charecterization 140
negative connotation 27, 51, 79
negative tonalities 160
neglect 94, 106, 170, 171
neutral phrasing 152
Nietzsche 2, 4
nightmare 53
non-human symbolism 175
nonstandard spelling
    and punctuation 60
nonsynchronous socialization 137
normalcy 47, 60
Novellentechnik 3
nucleus
    of society 167

objective style 113
official certifications 102
omnipresence of thematic 112
one-dimensional symbolism 26
opposite configurations 101
oppositive positivity 162
optimal limits 121
ordering of stories 134
origin
    of novellas 17
    of critical problems 1
original edition 4
original works in the collection 12
orthographic connotations 69

outer narrative 42, 46, 49, 100, 123, 126, 133, 144
outline of character 62, 68, 95
    of structure, style, thematic 114, 138
    of study approach 2
oversight
    by publisher 60
overtones
    of image 144
ownership 101
    rights of 141

painter 59
    Stifter as 9
pairing technique 59, 76, 101, 134
parabolic insertions 30, 112, 114, 124
paradox 41, 64, 68, 155
    in criticism 11
paraphrase 86
parental postures 171
partial text analyses 9
passage-by-passage analysis 18
passive constructions 25, 119, 127
past perfect, the 135
pathos 32
peasant rebellion 144
pedagogical motifs 17, 43
perceptual ambivalence 90
perceptual mosaic 122
periodical literature 14
personal fulfillment 53
personalization 27
personifications 114, 120, 126
Pflicht 63
philosophic variation
    of theme 69
philosophical overview in criticism 8, 12, 177
philosophical premise
    of stories 11
philosophical pronouncements 113
    in preface 4, 8
phonetic connotations 69
phrasing 33, 98, 152
pivotal figure 136
pivotal passage 28
pleasantness

    of tone, imagery 136
plethora of verbs 147
plot complication 132
plot lines 57
plots 17
    variety of 6
plural, the
    choice of 117
pluralistic world
    acceptance of 178
"poetic monotony" 12
point-counterpoint of imagery 63, 74, 151
polarity
    thematic 17, 146
political events of 1848 5
political unity 41
popularity
    of the collection 14
positive connotation 79
positive images 81, 92
positive tonalities 115, 160
possessive, the 79
    connotation of 119
preface, the 1-3, 7, 8, 11, 18, 20
prefiguration 58, 121, 124, 126, 142, 151
preponderance
    of impersonals 113
prestige 44, 99
preterite, the 135
preview
    narrational, thematic 123
prioritization
    compositional 177
    of values 120
problematical understanding of
    collection 177
professional identity 102
professional integrity 88
professional jealousy 105
prohibition 125, 156
proof of unity
    thematic 178
property 102, 141, 165
Prunk 100
pseudo-objective pronouncements 113

psycho-social flaw
    in *Hof* 16
psychological atmosphere 79
psychological boundary 163
psychological defensiveness 159
psychological equilibrium 171
psychological isolation
psychological make-up 101
psychological reintegration 52
psychological stress 164
publication
    date of collection 1
    political revolution before 7
publisher 60
    correspondence with 9
punctuation 60, 68, 134
punishment 35, 41

question of a literary series 111
quotation
    use of 24, 27, 29, 60, 75

"Rahmen" technique 112
Raphael 59
rapprochement 70
rare use
    of inanimate 120
"Rauh-Rinde" 123
reabsorption
    into society 50
reader, the 11, 23, 43, 50, 67, 77, 83, 96, 103, 114, 126, 135, 154, 167
reappearance
    and style 129
    of motif 81
recapitulation 54, 91, 152
Rechtschreibung 110
reciprocal relationship
    theme to structure 177
reconciliation 1, 52, 91, 105
recurrent motifs 91
reeducation 102
reevocation
    style of 130
references
    contemporary 12
    to earlier versions 12

reflexive 143, 49
Regierung 61
rehabilitation 36, 51
reiteration technique 26, 31, 50, 57, 64, 86, 109, 120, 131, 159
relief
    perspective 128
religious communality 45, 113
religious dimension 42
religious formulae 146
repetition 34
    of images 16, 115
    stylistic 16
    thematic 11
Requadt, Paul 17
resocialization 52
resolutions
    variety of 6
responsibility 5, 46, 102, 115, 148, 151
"resubjectivization" 99
retreat
    by author 112
reversed image 85
reversed polarity
    thematic 146
rewriting
    by Stifter 4
Richter, Ludwig
    illustrations by 4
rights 141
    of ownership 141
Rilke 4
rituals 62, 107
role-model 32
romantic conception of personality 13
rural life 133

Sabbath 6, 13
sacrifice 149, 152
Sagarra, Eda 3, 4
"sanfte Gesetz, das" 1
school 80, 90, 91, 101
secondary literature 177
    survey of 16
self-awareness 13, 39, 64, 66, 72
self-reproach 106

self-sacrificing effort 169
self-sufficiency 166
semi-integration 142
sentimentality 169
separateness 121, 129, 163, 173
sequence of paragraphs 89
series
    of images 138
    of paragraphs 141, 144, 150
    of works 111
shame 93
shifts
    of time frame, viewpoint 57
shyness 165
simile 145, 147
simultaneous depiction 57
simultaneous revelation, analysis 74
Sittlichkeit 110
Sjögren, Christine Oertel 16, 175
sketches
    narrative 130
slow moving plots 17
social animal
    man as 179
social continuum 9, 172
social dynamics 169
social impulses 170
social initiatives 101
social integration 62, 69, 99, 102, 109, 123, 131, 141
social limits 160
social prestige 99
social sanction 62
social skills 103
social welfare 109
socialized patterns 168
society
    and individual 9, 14
    natural orders of 13
solidarity 160, 166
solitude 99
sparing use
    of subjunctive 112
spatial values
    connotative 79
spelling 60
spirit and mind
    capacities of 58, 84

status 81, 147
Steffen, Konrad 7-10, 110
Stefl, Max 110
Stern, J. P. 14
Stifter criticism 2
    on collection 11
    tone and scope of 3
Stifter'schen Rechtschreibung 110
story-within-a-story 57, 94, 96, 103
stress 164, 172
structural analysis 177
structural arrangement 58, 69, 149, 171
structural balance 60
structural dissimilarities 113
structural form 114, 119
structural interaction
    with philosophical 158
structural juxtaposition 6, 146, 177
structural pairing 59, 72
structural peculiarities 57
structural, stylistic similarities 109
structural transition 60
structural variation 73
structural verticality 143
structural "pulling back"
    also stylistic and contextual 74
structure, style, and content
    interaction of 18, 67
Sture Mure 7, 10, 13, 16, 114
stylistic ambivalence 139
stylistic choices 6, 58, 69, 76, 154, 177
stylistic concentration
    of verbs 87
stylistic peculiarities 57
stylistic support for tone 84
stylistic variation 73
stylistic "pulling back"
    also structural 74
stylized use of comparative 76
subjunctive 59, 65-68, 72, 81, 95, 103, 112, 129, 132-134, 142, 150, 160, 171
success 95, 99, 104, 108, 109, 169, 173
superior initiative 147, 150
supraegoistic position 152

survey
    of criticism 2
suspension
    thematic 142
suspensive technique 73, 86, 159, 167
Swales, Martin 19, 21
symbolic ambiguity 87
symbolic limits 130, 161, 170
symbolic power 4
symbolic tales 138
symbolism 69, 175

tale-within-a-tale 33, 45
teacher 107
technical similarity
    of novellas 160
techniques
    compositional 6
temporal aspects
    of socialization 44
text analyses
    partial 9
textual balance 54
textual contrast 79
textual density 120
textual near-duplication 72
textual proofs
    in Aluf 12
textually debatable view
    by Sagarra 3
thematic antipode 26
thematic balance 45, 160
thematic common denominator 177
thematic complex 23, 24, 58, 109, 164
thematic configurations 8, 75
thematic density 48
thematic development 7, 101, 111, 167
thematic diffuseness 54
thematic extension 42
thematic focus 27, 40, 95, 157
thematic implementation
    of theory 11
thematic importance
    of frame narrative 5
thematic impulse

    and Stifter 21
thematic interplay
    compositional aspects of 10
    two components of 8
thematic interrelatedness
    of frame narrative 5
thematic questions
    outside "gentle law" 4
thematic sets
    for novellas 13
thematic substratum 86
thematic tension 29, 31, 46, 138
thematic variety 9, 13, 109
themes
    of integration and isolation 18
    Stifter and other 14
theoretical base
    of preface 11
theory
    of "gentle law" 11
thesis 26
    of "preface" 7
    of thematic interplay 18
three themes
    interplay of 18
    manifestations of 18
time 62, 70, 73, 93, 104
    inner 67
    narrated 143
time frames 57, 177
tonal ambivalence 72, 129
tonal underpinning
    of thematic 119
tone
    of criticism 3
    tragic, in the novellas 3
tragedy 142
    in the novellas 3
"tragic"
    characters 14
transcendence
    yearning for 8
transcultural socialization 125, 138, 140
transenvironmental socialization 121
transitional work
    Bunte Steine as a 17
"transsocializing" 166